A BOOK OF CHILDREN'S PARTIES

Helen Thomas was born in Manchester in 1930, one of five children. She was educated at the Convent School then at Parkfields Cedars Grammar School in Derby and went on to the University of Wales, where her father had become Professor of Metallurgy. She graduated in English and then spent a year in France working for the British Council before completing an Honours Degree in French. In 1951 she joined the John Lewis Partnership as a graduate trainee. In 1954 she married a fellow student and resigned from John Lewis in 1955 to have the first of her three children. She has since lived in Reading, Berkshire, where she combines domesticity with freelance writing and broadcasting interspersed, over the years, with the occasional television appearance, lectures, illustrating, teaching and translating French, library work and cooking for profit. *A Book of Children's Parties* is her first book, although she has had articles published in the *Guardian*, the *Observer*, *The Sunday Times* and IPC magazines and is currently working on a book of contemporary prayers due to be published in 1977 and a television series demonstrating a new way of communicating prayer. Her interests include religion, food, travel and the arts.

A BOOK OF CHILDREN'S PARTIES

HELEN THOMAS

Illustrated by Gunvor Edwards

PENGUIN BOOKS

Penguin Books Ltd, Harmondsworth, Middlesex, England
Penguin Books, 625 Madison Avenue, New York, New York 10022, U.S.A.
Penguin Books Australia Ltd, Ringwood, Victoria, Australia
Penguin Books Canada Ltd, 41 Steelcase Road West, Markham, Ontario, Canada
Penguin Books (N.Z.) Ltd, 182–190 Wairau Road, Auckland 10, New Zealand

—

First published 1976

—

Copyright © Helen Thomas, 1976

—

Made and printed in Great Britain by
Cox & Wyman Ltd,
London, Reading and Fakenham
Set in Monotype Baskerville

To Claire, Philippa and Richard

CONTENTS

INTRODUCTION

As our children grow up, most of us seem to get involved in parties almost without realizing it. The urge to celebrate a first baby's first birthday is naturally strong. We might mark the occasion by knocking up a sponge cake, sticking a candle on top and inviting a friend and her baby round. She may return the invitation, and from then on we are in the party business, off and on, for the next eighteen years.

This book is designed to help you give parties which you and the children can really enjoy. It deals mainly with activities for children between the ages of about four and twelve; but there are also some hints for entertaining teenagers successfully. The first section contains unconventional ideas for things to do, action parties which are much more interesting than the conventional sort. The second section contains more unconventional ideas, this time for things to eat, while the third gives nearly 100 games which should help more traditional parties to go with a swing.

In their first couple of years at primary school many children live in an absolute whirl of parties. At first parties are special and exciting, but all too quickly the novelty wears off and, although they always say they want to go, the children become almost bored, meeting the same group of friends, playing the same sort of games and eating the same sort of food. Because they are bored they behave badly and leave the hostess wounded and worn out by their apparent ingratitude.

This unfortunate attitude seems to be caused by the 'sameness' of most parties, and the solution to it lies in your own hands. You can't substitute other children for your children's friends, but you *can* introduce variety in what they do and what they eat.

I would suggest fairly conventional parties up to the age of six, preparing four or five games for before tea and four or five more for after. Between the ages of six and twelve, when this sort of party begins to pall, try out some of the action parties described in the first section. The idea of these is to organize some activity, such as carol singing, bob-a-job, puppet shows, cooking, which happens to appeal at that particular stage of the children's development. You do not need a large house or garden for any of these parties. Some of them require your taking the children out to a patch of grass, a park or a field, but most city dwellers nowadays can manage this. The majority of the action parties can be staged in any flat or small house providing you don't invite more children than you can accommodate. Much of the time will be taken up by a specific project, but after tea two or three games are usually a good idea to round off the occasion. From the age of twelve a lot of children seem to tire of parties for a year or two, perhaps gathering their strength for the highly demanding period of teenage parties.

It is only fair to warn you that, if your parties are a success, you are unlikely to get away with just one a year. All sorts of things can trigger them off – a long spell of fine weather, a long spell of bad weather, new friends, new acquisitions, new hobbies – so it is helpful to have up your sleeve a whole range of things to do.

Many children are surprisingly anxious about going to parties – particularly if they are not familiar with your house and with you. They are always pleased to be invited and keen to accept, but once dressed up and on the doorstep their nerve tends to fail. They feel shy and ill at ease. Action parties get off the ground straight away because the children are united by a common interest or activity, but conventional parties need a really good game to break the ice and dissolve self-consciousness (see games, pp. 133–142).

Children *like* to be organized, and to give a successful party you have to be prepared to spare a little time for planning in advance. This planning can be part of the pleasure. If your children really want a party, they will cooperate in the preparation and it will happily occupy them for a few days beforehand; if they are not all that keen, forget it until they are, or you will have to make all the running. At least some of the food should be things that children from the age of seven upwards can prepare or decorate. Get right away from the ubiquitous chipolatas, crisps and ice cream at this stage and plan some food which they will enjoy and remember and which will distinguish your party from all the others.

Invitations enhance the sense of anticipation and should go out about two weeks in advance. Cardboard stars, flowers or hearts inscribed by your children with coloured felt pens are more fun than costly printed ones. A request to 'R.S.V.P.' helps the hostess to plan and may instil the beginnings of a sense of social responsibility. Most of us do not have the space to entertain large groups of youngsters. If you have an average size house or flat, and three children of your own, it is better to limit the guests to seven at the most. State clearly what time they should come and what time the party will finish. Best to keep it fairly short – one and a half to two hours for the under sixes, about two and a half hours for an action party. This leaves enough time to achieve something but forestalls fatigue and fractiousness. Give a few details of the sort of action that is planned and some idea of what to wear. Although children love to receive their own mail through the post, this has become so expensive that it seems better to let your children spend an afternoon putting invitations through the letter boxes of those who live near by. Avoid handing them out at school, as this can spark off unhappiness and jealousy in those who are not invited.

Around Christmas particularly one is tempted to put crackers on the table, but they cost a lot if they are not going to be too abysmally disappointing and there are less extravagant and more original ways of making it look festive. If you want to put a little present at each place, then in winter you can make snowballs by wrapping the gifts in cotton wool, spraying them with glittery 'frost' and sticking in a minute sprig of holly; and in summer you can wrap the present in big leaves, tie them with raffia and tuck a couple of fresh flowers into the top.

A few prizes for some of the games are a good idea, but remember that they should be suitable for a boy or a girl, while jokey prizes which everyone will enjoy are good for cheering up those who do not actually win. If you speed your guests on their way with parting gifts, keep them small and inexpensive – tiny notebooks, bath cubes, a bar of chocolate, a pencil sharpener or rubber – prettily wrapped and named.

Teenage parties demand a few words of special warning. Unless you want the whole teenage community of the county turning up, you *must* issue invitations and ask your guests to bring them. There is no easy way to prevent duplication but, if you put the name of the guest and a number on each, you can have a check list pinned up by the front door. News of a party spreads like wildfire and many young people nowadays think that to present themselves on the doorstep armed with a bottle entitles them to admission. Teenagers rarely care what they eat as long as there is something around to nibble. To prevent recrimination and regret on the morning after, prepare the place as though for a siege: roll up the carpets and protect decent surfaces with thick layers of newspaper covered with dark cloths; remove anything removable from walls, shelves, windowsills and tables; replace ornaments with ashtrays and bowls of sand and yet more ashtrays even if your children swear blind that nobody smokes. The place may well look dreadful to your civilized eye, but the guests will not even notice. Maximum noise with minimum illumination seems to be the ideal.

So, parties are for fun. They are not meant to prove anything, outdo anybody or necessitate expense, exhaustion and chaos. They won't *be* fun unless you take pleasure in preparing them and seeing them through. If you can inject a little originality into them, you will be storing up memories for your children and their friends which they, in turn, will want to emulate. Perhaps this book will help you.

WHAT TO DO

This first section will give you some ideas for parties which are different because they have a theme, and for most of the time the children will not just be playing an assortment of games but will be engaged in a particular activity.

The first twenty-two ideas, listed in alphabetical order, are for parties which can be staged at any time of the year. Then there are ten themes associated with certain seasons, listed in chronological order.

1. ACTION PARTIES

Animal Lovers' Party (age four upwards)

Nearly all children are fond of animals and will love a party which encourages this interest and affection – particularly if they are not able to keep pets of their own.

There are several possible ways of giving an animal lovers' party. If you live near a zoo or animal sanctuary, you can take them all on a visit with either a picnic tea or tea at home afterwards. But the cost of keeping and feeding animals has risen so dramatically that the entrance fee to zoos has unfortunately become something of a deterrent, unless you can get a substantial reduction for a party.

However, many towns have an annual cat, dog or pet show. Our town hall, for example, houses a Siamese Cat

Show every autumn. Here, for a few pence admission, can be seen a wide assortment of kittens and cats and all the latest developments in breeding with tabby, ginger and lavender extremities (or 'points' as they are technically called). Your group of children can happily spend a good hour at such a show, admiring the animals and watching the judges at work before returning home for tea.

If your children and some of their friends are lucky enough to have pets of their own, you can take your courage in both hands and have a pets party. It would obviously be courting chaos to have a Great Dane, an Alsatian and a Labrador visiting an average house or flat at one time – so exercise a degree of caution. Small dogs which can be kept on leads in the house and which won't make a clean sweep of the tea table with one wag of a tail are perfectly acceptable and are, in fact, easier to control than cats, which tend to disappear without trace or barricade themselves under some impossibly low piece of furniture. Pets in cages such as birds, mice, hamsters, gerbils, guinea pigs and rabbits are ideal, providing the children or their parents can transport them. Tortoises, of course, can be very entertaining, but do not consider offering house room to any of the other reptiles or to birds of prey.

Cages can be ranged in a garage, shed, porch or hallway – you can cover the floor with newspaper or old dust cloths. Children are able to talk authoritatively and unselfconsciously about their pets – what they eat, what they like, what they do – and will enjoy putting them through their paces in turn.

Once interest in the animals has worn thin, have tea and a selection of suitable games.

Horse lovers qualify for a party of their own and there are suggestions for these on p. 28.

Bicycle Ride (age nine upwards)

It is best to make a few discreet inquiries among parents before you broach this idea. You need to know which children have roadworthy bikes (and the parents' idea of 'roadworthy' may differ from the children's), whether they can ride them safely (again get the parents' opinion) and whether they are allowed on the road on them (parents' ruling final). You need a bike yourself and you need a willing friend with a bike. Then plan your route.

The ideal is a two- or three-mile loop involving only left turns along quiet lanes that are not too narrow. If possible, aim for a friend with a large garden or garage who would not mind you depositing with her beforehand a box of fruit or soft drinks and a big rug – but keep this part secret.

When the children first arrive, and whenever necessary later, get them to lean their bikes up separately against different walls, trees, fences. No double (or treble or quadruple) parking, nor bicycles lying on top of each other on the ground, or you will end up with tangled pedals, broken spokes, oily trousers and irate parents.

Set off in single file with an adult leading and an adult bringing up the rear. Keep up a brisk, even pace. When you get to your friend's house, surprise them all by singing out 'Turn left into this garden,' and there, spread out in the shade or in the garage if it's raining, will be rest and refreshment. Enjoy half an hour of I spy and some other word games before cycling back to washes, cool drinks and something to eat which is light but sustaining, such as iced shrimp soup, cheese aigrettes, ham mousse and fruit.

Have some quieter games after tea and, if you have enough space and your guests are sufficiently proficient, you could finish up with a session of bicycle polo.

Bob-a-job (age ten upwards)

Borrow an idea from the Boy Scouts and have a bob-a-job session in aid of some charity of the children's own choosing or a local cause which appeals to them. Since 'bobs' (shillings) have gone for ever, I suppose 'a task for ten pence' would be more in keeping with the times.

Spread the word around the neighbours, so that they will reserve some little chore for the children to do. If you live in an area where most people are out at work, then have your party on a Saturday. People tend to go out, put their feet up or have visitors in the afternoons so it is best to invite the children to meet at your house at about 11. Then, over a glass of fruit juice and some biscuits, they can each make out a list on a post card of the sort of jobs they are prepared to tackle. This is a great help to the householder, who very often – although perfectly willing to cooperate – cannot think of a suitable job, and it also means that the children are less likely to take on things which are really beyond them. Here are some suggestions:

1 Shopping
2 Delivering messages
3 Cleaning shoes
4 Walking dogs (small ones)
5 Sweeping and scrubbing porches
6 Trimming lawn edges
7 Weeding
8 Sweeping paths
9 Polishing silver or brass
10 Raking up leaves
11 Watering the garden
12 Cleaning windows
13 Cleaning outside windowsills
14 Washing up

Some children will want to hunt in pairs and some prefer to work alone. Send them on their way and tell them to be back at about one o'clock for lunch.

Prepare a substantial meal, as they will have worked pretty hard – perhaps soup (hot or cold depending on the time of year), apple sausage roll with potato cakes and lemon water ice, or soup followed by a great bowl of kedgeree and then vanilla ice cream. After lunch count up the earnings so far and compare notes. This may give some of them ideas for jobs which they can add to their lists. Then take a vote as to whether they want to go off again while people are still at home and do another hour. Chances are that they will and this gives you time to clear up. Fix a deadline – certainly not later than three o'clock – and make it clear that anyone who is tired can come back earlier. After all, it's not supposed to be slave driving.

When they are all reassembled you can have a grand reckoning of the proceeds. If it is possible to arrange for a representative of the cause for which you have been working to call about this time and receive the money, this will round off proceedings in a most satisfactory way. Have a drink and a biscuit and then a few undemanding games before the children go home.

Bus Ride (ages four to nine)

It is surprising how many children have never been as far as the termini of the bus route on which they live and this can provide an entertaining afternoon for a younger age group.

It is only fair on the bus company and the general public to choose a reasonably quiet time, so meet at your house at about 2.30 p.m. Bribe a friend or one of the mothers to come along and help you, and divide the group between you.

If the children can write (the spelling they use is incidental), give them each a pencil and a plain post card or jotting pad with their name on, and take some extra ones with you. If they are not yet at the writing stage, you and your friend will have to act as writers for each group.

Decide beforehand what category of things they are going to watch for on the way, depending on whether the bus route is urban, suburban or rural. Here are some suggestions for items you could collect. You might choose one for the outward journey and another for the return journey:

Urban   1 Different sorts of shops
          2 Objects made of metal
          3 Different vehicles

	4	Red things
	5	Green things
	6	Uniforms
	7	Car parks
Suburban	1	House names
	2	Delivery vans
	3	Pets
	4	Letter boxes
	5	Telephone boxes
	6	Police telephones
	7	Bus stops
Rural	1	Flowers
	2	Trees
	3	Animals and birds
	4	Milestones
	5	Farm machinery
	6	Signposts
	7	Different crops

Explain to the children what they are looking for and tell them that whenever they see something in this category they must either keep it to themselves and write it down or call it out to their writer but not so loudly as to annoy the other passengers.

When the bus arrives shepherd them on to the upper deck – if there is one. Seat half on one side of the bus and half on the other at the back, so that they see different things. There will be some reshuffling when most of them decide they want to be on the opposite side or have to sit beside somebody else. You may be able to buy round tickets; if not, book to the terminus and then say you have changed your minds and want tickets home again.

After tea you can compare lists and award little prizes for the individuals or group with the longest list of legitimate entries, followed by a variety of quiet and lively games before they leave.

Caravan Party (ages five to nine)

Nowadays more and more families seem to have a caravan parked alongside the house and although it may be 'out of bounds' normally for the children it is a wonderful stand-by if a party you have planned is rained off, or just as a sort of 'playing at house' party for a group of not too rough guests. Make your preparations, put your own children in charge and keep out of the way.

Children are fascinated by things in miniature and the things to eat and drink you hide away in cupboards for them to find should all be tiny, for example, little bottles of fruit juice with medicine glasses or coffee cups from which to drink it. If you cannot buy those miniature loaves of brown bread which cut into slices about two inches square, stamp sandwiches into little rounds, triangles, stars and crescents with pastry cutters. Have cocktail sausages, bite-size vol-au-vents, miniature crackers, minute biscuits and individual iced cakes with names piped on in contrasting colours.

Put some small-size patience cards out on the table, turn on a transistor radio placed out of reach on top of a cupboard, then lock the door and give the children the key to let themselves in.

To start with they will want to explore and try the beds and run the taps (if they run) and examine the loo (if there is one) – so be prepared for all that. Brief your own children with ideas for a few games like link names or Simon says, which they will doubtless play stretched out on the beds, then some simple card games like beg-of-my-neighbour and snap.

They won't be able to resist the tea for long so this party had better start at about 3.30, and once the food is demolished and the washing-up done – after a fashion – they will probably explode from the caravan. By that time you should be standing by with some good lively games ready.

Car-Spotting Party (age seven upwards)

Boys from the age of about six upwards seem to dote on cars for years. Some girls will enjoy joining in a car-spotting party too, but they are not usually quite so knowledgeable about the different makes of car.

If you live right on a busy road, spotting can quite well be done by ranging chairs along upstairs windows and spacing the children along them. However, they will get bored unless the road is really busy with a car passing every minute or two. Otherwise take them on a fine day to a pedestrian bridge over a road or motorway, a busy junction or just a main road where there is a bank or benches at a safe distance from the traffic.

Each child needs a small notebook and a pencil. Before you set out, get them to rule five columns on each page and write headings on the first page as a guide. For instance: 1, Type of car; 2, Registration number; 3, Colour; 4, Number of people; 5, Any other features (e.g. large dog with head out of window, red number plates, learner driver, radio aerial, etc.).

Once at your vantage point, they can either work individually or in pairs. About an hour on the job will be enough, then back for tea and afterwards you can compare notes. Award, for example, one point for every car correctly noted and two points for each valid extra feature. Majority rule will have to be the order of the day – for instance, if nine of them say that the fifth car was a blue Simca then the tenth who swears it was a blue Renault is probably wrong. Give prizes for the first three and then arrange a few games to complete the afternoon.

Cooking Party (age eight upwards)

For your own sanity and your guests' safety keep this party small. However spacious your kitchen, six is the maximum

24

number you will be able to supervise without too much stress. Of course the party need not be restricted to girls – boys who like to cook are often very good at it. Their approach, however, is quite different. Girls will agonize for minutes over cracking an egg against the edge of a basin while boys will gaily smash it in the palm of their hand against the side and, if one or two eggs sail out of their shells and skim across the table on to the floor, it will not reduce the boys to tears but to paroxysms of mirth. Once their efforts are in the oven, some will sit back and relax until the cooking is complete and they can tuck in, while others will bustle about tidying the kitchen and washing up.

Tea parties are best on the whole, as the business of co-ordinating timing matters less with tea food and it is difficult to gauge how slow a child cook will be. Ask them to come round at about 2.30 and then decide between you what you will make.

You will find plenty of simple recipes (the starred ones) in the cookery section of this book but you might try a menu of: bacon rolls, stuffed eggs, cheese biscuits, fruit scones, Scotch pancakes and chocolate crisps, with perhaps a big cake as your more professional contribution. The children may prefer to tackle one item on their own or may derive moral support from working in pairs on two different items.

Quite a lot of mixing bowls and spoons will be required. Things which they will all need to use – such as flour and weighing scales – should be in an accessible central position. Perch yourself on a stool beside the cooker, so that you can keep a close watch on everything and tell them to come to *you* if they need help, so that you don't have to leave your post.

As they finish, they can take their turn to wash up their own utensils in one big bowl of water and once everything is safely out of the oven you can all take time off to play a few games.

When tea time approaches they can lay the table, decorate it with flowers and leaves and arrange their productions on the dishes of their choice. This is one time when they will *really* appreciate what they are eating and, if there are a few things left over, you might let them take them home to impress their own families.

Cricket Party   (age eight upwards)

Any group of children currently keen on cricket will enjoy this. It is varied to circumstances and could either involve an expedition to watch a village, school or county match with a picnic lunch or tea, or taking a group (minimum six, maximum twenty-two) to a park, pitch or field to play themselves. Alternatively you could start by watching a match and, after a picnic lunch or tea, stage your own. Cricket is a slow-moving game and, unless the match you watch is absolutely first rate, the passive role of spectator is not one that suits some children for long stretches.

If you only have a small group, you can manage on the very basic requirements of a bat, two stumps and a ball. A cricket ball or very hard rubber ball are best since a tennis or lighter ball travels so far that the fielders get tired of chasing it.

If it is not easy to take a picnic, provide a bag of fruit to eat at half time, play for a little longer and come back home to iced soup, stuffed mushrooms, quiche, home-made ices (pp. 62, 82, 83 and 123).

Fancy Dress Party   (age three upwards)

Nearly all children love dressing up but a straight fancy dress party can sometimes cause problems and anxiety. Some families have great trunk-loads of glamorous old bits and pieces from which the children can help themselves, and some mothers are wizards with a sewing machine and enjoy the challenge of whipping up something out of nothing; but others have not the time, energy or imagination to bother and so the poor child is left in a dilemma.

If you happen to know that the children possess or have access to costumes (such as national costumes or outfits they have had for dancing or shows of some sort), you can go ahead in the conventional way. But if you think that some of the children might have difficulties, there are lots of alternatives which can lead to painless fancy dress.

The children can come in their ordinary clothes and be presented, on arrival, with a carrier bag or old pillow case full of things for them to put on top – a hat, a blouse, cardigan or jacket, a skirt or trousers and eccentric extras like old spectacles, dangly beads, feather boas, bags, boots and scarves. Mix the funny things fairly with the unexceptional ones – nobody wants to feel they look more ridiculous than the rest.

Or you can select a theme consisting of clothes which you know any family would have. For example, give a Tramps party, inviting them to come in the oldest, tattiest, weirdest assortment of things they can find and giving a prize to the wildest of all. A Funny Uniform party is quite successful. For this the guests have to put together any improbable combination of uniforms – school, army, boy scout, girl guide, nurse's – whatever they can get hold of. A Grown Up party is one of the easiest, for every child has bigger brothers, sisters or parents from whom they can borrow long skirts, earrings, car coats, umbrellas, hats and caps. A Sportman's party is another fairly safe one, for most families have some football, tennis or golfing gear which can be appropriated; or a Pyjama party, for which they wear dressing-gowns, night-gowns or pyjamas as they like.

Slightly older children will have a go at devising costumes if you pick a suitably easy theme such as Monsters (black cloaks made from curtains or skirts, blackened faces, terrible teeth cut from orange or lemon rind) or Fairies (anything pretty and floating with wands and wings and coronets of flowers to taste) or 'Diddy' People (with feather dusters as 'tickle sticks' and trousers and shirts padded out with cushions to make them as wide as they are high).

This is one action party which needs a good ice breaker to

start it off, as young guests are liable to feel shy and inhibited in their unaccustomed clothes. Once the ice is broken, you can award different prizes for the outfits (funniest, prettiest, cleverest, etc.) and then let the children discard anything that is cumbersome, uncomfortable or particularly fragile, so that they can relax and enjoy the rest of the games without anxiety.

Football Party (age six upwards)

Such is the extraordinary popularity of football that you can legitimately stage this party at any time of the year and it need not even be restricted to boys.

All you have to do is to take the children and a good ball to a park or field where there is plenty of room, divide them into two teams, mark out goal posts and blow a whistle. If you are acting as referee, it is as well to have a vague idea of the rules.

Half an hour each way is probably enough. If it is summer they will be boiling hot and if it is winter *you* will be deep frozen at the end of an hour.

Amble home to remove dirty boots – which they leave in the porch – have showers or jolly good washes and tuck into a hearty meal with lots of drinks followed by some word games or pencil and paper games played casually curled up in armchairs or stretched out on the carpet.

Horse Lovers' Party (age nine upwards)

Many girls and quite a few boys go through a period of passionate devotion to horses. If you have one such child in the family, he or she will be overjoyed at the idea of a horse lovers' party for like-minded friends. Just what form this will take must depend on what is available in your neighbourhood.

Within a few miles of us we have two stud farms and three

riding schools and my children have one or two friends who are lucky enough to keep their own ponies. Other towns, of course, have racecourses and polo grounds and you can always track down gymkhanas and horse shows in the summer and meets in the winter.

If you have a stud farm within reasonable distance, call round, telephone or write (enclosing a stamped, addressed envelope) beforehand to ask if you may bring a small party of well-behaved (hopefully!) horse lovers. The one nearest to us has an enormous stable yard with about twenty-five stables. Often each stable houses a mare and a foal. There are usually one or two stable lads (who can be male or female, young or not so young), who are happy to chat, answer the children's questions and introduce them to the animals. Sometimes all the horses are turned out into the water meadows opposite where they are a joy to watch. You should not attempt to feed them, because these are often very valuable creatures and the owners of the stud will rightly object and there is always the danger that fingers will get accidentally nipped. If it is a fine day, you could take a picnic, or come back home again for tea and some games.

Friendly local riding schools offer several possibilities. For a small group of younger children some schools will let you hire a docile old pony for an hour which you and your party can lead around quiet lanes taking it in turns to have a ride. Or, if funds will run to it, you can book ponies for a few children who have already done a bit of riding and then the school will supervise them for you.

If any of your children's friends have ponies, their parents might give permission for them to bring the ponies round and – under your supervision – let your guests practise grooming, saddling up, mounting and perhaps allow each child a short ride.

Racecourses and polo grounds are not usually considered children's territory, but the atmosphere, the speed and the dazzling beauty of the horses are guaranteed to make any hippophile's heart beat faster; so they are well worth a visit if they are within striking distance and if the entrance fee is not too exorbitant. Choose the cheapest enclosure. It is just as much fun.

A gymkhana, of course, provides a lovely picnic outing for a group of horse lovers. Apart from what is going on in the ring, there are all the peripheral activities as people unbox horses, groom them and saddle and warm them up.

Local newspapers publish details of meets in the area. Since they usually move off in the middle of the morning, you could make your party a lunch-time one after following the hunt on foot for a while. The excitement, the glamour, the bustle, the noise, the ebullience of the hounds and the eccentricity of the participants can all be highly diverting.

Lunch-Time Concerts (age ten upwards)

Most sizeable towns now put on lunch-time concerts in the autumn and winter months. They are often held in the town hall or art gallery and their two great attractions, for our purpose, are that they are short (usually about forty minutes) and they are free.

Music has become a very important feature in schools. Children are encouraged to learn any instrument that appeals to them, and most instruments are available for hire at a nominal fee.

Once any of your children and their friends embark on this, they will be interested to hear a professional or a group of professionals performing on the same instruments. When my eldest child took up the oboe, I took her and five friends to hear Leon Goossens. None of them had even been to a concert before and they were totally absorbed.

In our town the concerts start at 1.10 and finish at about 1.45. Although most musically orientated schools would allow you to take the children out of school to the concert and miss some of the afternoon's lessons, this does not give you much time; so, if the idea is to build a little celebration around the performance, it would be better to settle for one during the school holidays.

Office workers who attend bring their sandwiches, but children are not awfully good at surreptitious picnicking, so invite them to meet at your house in time to have a snack (e.g. iced soup and cheese biscuits or hot soup and rolls) before going down to the concert hall. Try to get there in time to have seats near the front – of the balcony, if there is one – so that the children's attention is easily held. Return home for the rest of lunch, perhaps ham loaves with salad and a fruit flan. Afterwards you could have some lively games and, at minimal expense, you will have furnished them with a rewarding experience.

Matchbox Filling   (age seven upwards)

Because children love tiny things and love hoarding, they always enjoy a competition to see who can cram the largest number of things into a matchbox. It demands imagination, ingenuity and perseverance.

Send out invitations a week beforehand and invite the children to start filling matchboxes there and then, for a prize will be awarded for the highest number of original items. As they put things into the box, they must list them, since it is much easier to start by checking the list than the almost invisible items it enumerates and, if in doubt, proof can always be demanded. The potential maximum runs into over three *hundred* and, when you think in mind-boggling terms of a grain of sugar, a tea leaf, a crumb, a cat hair, a wisp of cotton or a soap flake, you can see why!

So they will arrive with matchboxes bulging at the seams and reams of paper listing the contents. If possible, give each child a tray or a big cardboard lid; otherwise when they finally open the box many of the items will disappear for ever into your carpet.

Start by asking each child how many things he has listed and then ask the child with the longest list to read it out slowly item by item. Everybody who has the same crosses it off. Those who still have uncancelled items then read them out and duplicates are again deleted. This all takes a nice long time because the children spend ages locating entries on their individual lists.

In the end you will be left with several children who each have a few original items that nobody else has thought to include. The one who originally had the longest list may well have the largest number still unchallenged. If so, give him the top prize and award the second and third prizes to the runners up.

Tea next and then some active games with a few more prizes to cheer those who collected assiduously but were not among the winners.

Nature Walk   (age nine upwards)

Some advance research and hoarding are essential for this. The ideal is to earmark a circular route of about one and a half miles in length either from your house or from a convenient bus stop. It should include country lanes, a wood, an open field and, if possible, a stream or pond.

As each child arrives give him a carrier bag (preferably a polythene one) with his name on to prevent arguments after tea. Do not let rain or winter weather deter you, providing the children are properly dressed. Explain that this is an exercise in observation and that they are to look out for and collect *one* specimen of as many different sorts of natural things like grasses, leaves, buds, seed pods and flowers as they can find, as well as treasures like oak apples, bones, cones, feathers, pretty stones, fossils, sheep's wool, skeleton leaves. If you have selected a safe walk there is no need to supervise them very closely, although you must of course go along.

When you get back home, muddy boots and shoes will probably have to be discarded at the door and a queue formed for hand washing while you heat up some soup or drinking-chocolate to go with the food in case anybody feels cold.

After tea settle them around a big table or allocate each one a small table or a corner of uncarpeted floor. Give each a large shallow box lid, a pen, some glue, Sellotape and pins. While you wash up, ask them to fix their spoils as attractively as possible into the box lid and to write in the names of as many of them as they can, together with anything else they know about them. When they have all finished they can set their work on the table and clear up their rubbish while you judge for variety, presentation and amount of information. First, second, third and then equal fourth prizes for the rest are probably desirable.

Have a few restful games until it is time to go home and, when they leave, give them back their carrier or polythene bags so that they can slide their efforts in and take them home without the whole lot blowing away.

Old People's Party (age six upwards)

Combine the kindness inherent in most children with their pleasure in showing off to stage an entertainment for some of the lonely old people in the neighbourhood.

You may know some old folk who live locally whom you could invite to your house. Consult the vicar about this. Alternatively, if you live anywhere near an old people's home, contact the Matron and ask her if she thinks a small group would like to come round to be entertained by the children and given tea. However, many old people are often some-what loth to be winkled out of their everyday setting, so you and the Matron may decide that it would be better to take a few children round to the home. Find out what would be a suitable time and approximately how many residents will be present.

You will not in that case be giving the old people tea, although an inexpensive but pretty present for each would be welcomed. Old ladies appreciate things which smell nice and your own children could prepare some scented oranges for them, which double as moth deterrents. These are very simple but need at least a week in a warm airing cupboard to dry out. Choose medium oranges with thinnish skins, and stick cloves into them, leaving clear tracks for ribbon. Tie the ribbon round and make a loop on top for hanging, then leave to dry out. Other presents, for ladies or gentlemen, could be home-made sweets tied up in coloured paper with a ribbon, a miniature pot of jam or honey, a small tin of home-made biscuits or a tiny posy or buttonhole.

Ask the children to congregate at your house early in the afternoon and then prepare a short, lively concert – somebody will be able to play the recorder, someone will know a poem, someone will be able to dance and the whole group is sure to know a few songs. If the old people are visiting you, after performing, the children can serve them tea where they sit in their armchairs (to simplify this, prepare a plate for each person with a few sandwiches, a couple of biscuits and a slice of cake) but be sure everybody has a table handy on which to rest cups and saucers. It is probably safer and more comfortable for the children if they can have their tea around a table in the same room. The old people will derive real pleasure from just watching them and listening to their chatter.

If, on the other hand, you have decided it is better to visit the home, do the concert, hand out the presents and come back for tea. The children will be gratified to have been able to do something for somebody else.

Picnic Party (age four upwards)

We tend to think of picnics as summertime things, but some of the most disappointing picnics I have had with my family have been on grey chilly days in the summer months, whereas some of the best have been on clear, sparkling winter days.

Whatever time of year, you need a good open space. For a summer picnic it is lovely if you can find a field where there is a stream or pond, and for a winter picnic room to race around is essential and the possibility of lighting a fire a wonderful asset. You can picnic perfectly well in parks but, if you want to use a farmer's land, you must get his permission first, particularly, of course, if you hope to light a fire.

There is always a good deal to transport for a picnic. If you are going most of the way by car, this is no problem but, if you are travelling on foot, on bicycles or by public transport, divide the load out as fairly as possible.

For a winter picnic you must all be warmly clothed and take some kindling and a couple of Thermoses of hot soup or chocolate. Traditional fare like sausages and potatoes takes a long time to cook properly on an open fire, so pre-cook them for a winter picnic or serve things like baked beans or stew which you heat up and eat with spoons straight from the pan. For pudding parkin is nice. While the fire gets going, have lots of warming, racy games and some more after you have eaten. Take kites if it is windy. If there is snow, you can have snowball fights, sledge, slide and even make an igloo (*not* too close to the fire!) when the snow is deep and crisp enough to stick together.

One hopes that at summer picnic parties the problem will be to keep things cool. Show the children how to submerge bottles of cold drinks in the stream and alternate strenuous and sedentary games. Avoid boring sandwiches and provide big quiches, individual pots of rice salad and teaspoons, cakes, fruit and hard-boiled eggs with the children's names written on them with coloured felt pens.

Tidying up must be a combined operation and all paper, plastic, glass and metal refuse taken home with you.

Puppet Party (ages six to seven)

While your children are at the stage of enjoying glove, finger or string puppets, have a puppet party and invite everyone who has any puppets to bring them along.

There is no need to be deterred because you have not got a proper puppet theatre. A serving-hatch can be used, or a table in a bay window with the curtains fixed around it, or even a large grocery box between two chairs with the top cut away for string puppets or the bottom cut away for hand puppets.

It will get the ball rolling if your own children – or your eldest with a good friend – devise a little play with their puppets; then volunteers can be invited to continue the story or to start a new tale by introducing their own puppets. Have some music available if possible.

Plan a few energetic games for before tea, and afterwards the children can try making finger puppets out of large peanut shells. Crack the shells in half across the middle and draw faces on the halves with felt pens. Felt or paper hats and wool hair can be added for extra effect.

Put on a Play (age seven upwards)

There are several different ways of doing this and which will be most successful depends on how old and how extrovert your group is. Young children will not learn or remember lines, so they are best left to extemporize the actual dialogue to a simple story you have devised, or base a play on a nursery story they all know well. Rather older children may enjoy writing a simple play with your cooperation, and a more sophisticated group may like to track down a short play in the library and produce it properly.

Then you have to decide whether you are going to put the play on solely for the enjoyment of the children, or for the entertainment of parents and friends, or in aid of some cause so that you will charge for admission.

About four rehearsal sessions in the week beforehand is probably enough. Production will be simple, anyway, and you don't want the children to get stale. If they have to learn parts, of course, they will also have to do some homework.

Reward their efforts with a bumper tea or supper party afterwards and they will have thoroughly enjoyed the whole venture.

Swimming Party (age four upwards)

The lucky few who own a swimming-pool already know about the pitfalls and pleasures associated with having a group of children round to swim.

If you don't live near the sea or a suitable safe lake, stream or river, there probably is a reasonable swimming-pool close enough for an excursion there to be quite feasible.

Older children, of course, do not really need to be taken by you provided they have already learned to swim and there are lifeguards and supervision at the pool. However, they may need your initiative (and cash!) to organize a party.

For younger children it is a rare treat. You must limit yourself to about six and, if you are going to a public swimming-pool, choose a quiet time when they won't be swamped by school parties. Some of the newer pools have really shallow, separate areas for tiny children. Obviously you will have to take the plunge with them but, since the water is usually kept very warm and will only be about thigh-deep on you, this is no great penance. If there is no separate area for very small children, it is best not to take anybody under seven because they are liable to get splashed, pushed and panicked by bigger children jumping in over their heads.

Open-air pools with picnic-inviting grass alongside mean your party is ready made. The actual swimming, jumping in and diving can be relieved by sessions of water polo and pig-in-the-middle, which are undemanding and highly enjoyable. If a picnic is not possible, then it's back home to tea and a few games and you will have done a good day's work!

Train Ride (ages five to nine)

When my son was about five, his idea of heaven was a ride in a train. Casual questions to his mates established that few of them, in these car-ridden days, had ever been in a train, so they thought it a wonderful idea for a party.

Make some inquiries and find a little local train that stops at every station and from which you can alight about fifteen miles from home. Congregate either at the local station or at your house, whichever is more convenient, at about three o'clock. Take a picnic tea with you to eat in a field when you arrive or, if the worst comes to the worst weather-wise, in the waiting-room. The waiting-rooms in little country stations are usually deserted and often surprisingly homely.

Return by train or bribe one or two fathers to come and rescue you all by car at about five and whisk you home again.

Train Spotting (ages eight to twelve)

This is not, as is generally supposed, an exclusively male occupation. Many girls enjoy it too. Where you go to do it will again depend on where you live. If you have a fairly busy stretch of track or a junction near by, you can take a rug to a safe part of the bank and do it from there. If not, you may have to go to the station, buy platform tickets and get well out of the way at the end of some platform. Everybody will need notebooks and pencils.

Do not confine yourselves to noting engine numbers. There are lots of other things to be observed and noted, e.g. number of coaches, whether there is a dining-car, time of arrival and departure, number of first-class compartments. All this can form the basis of a competition after tea – to see who has observed most about each train. In the gaps between trains they can note down everything they can see beginning with the letters 't', 'r', 'a', 'i', 'n', try sketching signal boxes, etc.

Don't stay too long – an hour is plenty, because you still have to get them back home, finish the preparations for tea and let them tuck in before you start the train spotters' competition and organize a few games before they leave.

Treasure Hunt (age seven upwards)

Treasure hunts are tremendous fun and terribly exciting for children. So great is their excitement, though, that once they have found a clue they hardly ever remember to leave it, never mind hide it exactly as they found it. The leaders may have a lovely time but for the rest, trailing in their wake, the whole thing can become a great bore.

To avoid this, divide the children into twos or threes and allot a colour to each group. Those whose colour is pink must only take clues written on pink paper. It means more advance preparation for you because you have to devise a trail for each group, but it will work and there will be no disappointments.

Hand the first clue to them and number all of the clues so that they don't miss any out. Clues can take them all over the house and garden and even along the same side of the road in which you live, providing you are out in the street to watch the younger ones. Older children who know the area and are quite used to crossing quiet roads can go all over the immediate neighbourhood, which is even more fun and takes a good deal longer. For maximum exercise and maximum time consumption, spread them as widely as possible. The first clue, for instance, could take them down to the shed at the bottom of the garden ('This is where the wheelbarrow sleeps') and the second – hidden in the wheelbarrow – out to the front gate ('Number 15'). You have to gear the clues to suit the ages of the children, but make them puzzle over each one a little. Each group should have about ten clues to solve before coming upon their treasure, which can be bags of golden (chocolate) sovereigns or little gifts like bath cubes, pencil sharpeners, rubbers, tins of bubbles.

The racing about and the excitement will make them welcome cold drinks and ices with their tea, followed perhaps by some quieter pencil-and-paper games.

2. SEASONAL ACTION PARTIES

Twelfth Night Party (ages six to twelve)

Twelfth Night – or Epiphany – is on 6 January, twelve days after Christmas. Unless you are lucky enough to have snow, it tends to be a bleak time. The excitement of Christmas has evaporated, but the children are still on holiday from school. The decorations which went up in such a frenzy of anticipation now look tired and reproachful. The weather is usually too uninviting for much outdoor activity, so it is a thoroughly good idea to dispel the sense of anti-climax with preparations for a party which will end the school holidays on a high note.

This is the Feast Day which commemorates the arrival of the Three Wise Men in Bethlehem to greet the infant Jesus. Children love the Christmas story and in the week before the party you can, with the cooperation of your own children, devise a very simple play on this theme. The amount of speech and action must be geared to the age of the group of children involved, but the number of words they have to remember should be minimal.

Having decided on the outline of the play, you must then agree on who could fill which role – who can play the recorder, who can sing, who would be happiest off stage and ushering – and specify each child's part on his invitation in order to prevent bedlam when they arrive. Invite the children for 2.30 to prepare the play, and the parents for 4.30, to see it and take them home again.

Probably the play will be staged in the living-room, as this tends to be the largest and warmest area, but if you have a fairly spacious hallway with stairs consider that, because the stairs make good seats for the spectators and you will have more choice of exits and entrances.

You and your children will be able to devise a little play to suit your house and the talent available, but here is a suggested scenario to start you off. Begin in darkness with perhaps a solitary recorder playing 'Away in a Manger' or 'Silent Night'. One standard lamp or table lamp could then be switched on to reveal Mary (swathed in blue bedspread, curtain, cloak or bath towel) and Joseph (in similar brown, dark green or grey), with a large baby doll and a crib. They can chat together about the baby, the cold, whether Joseph ought to collect more firewood, and then fade back into the darkness.

In another corner of the room the Three Wise Men are now illuminated by a second lamp. In contrast to the first group they are brightly cloaked and wear dazzling crowns. Above them is a large cardboard star which is sprayed with glitter and which can be slung on a string. If your room is suitable, it can be towed very slowly across towards the first group on a pulley system by some child off stage. The Wise

Men discuss this strange star and decide to follow it bearing peace offerings of gold, frankincense and myrrh. They travel slowly and with difficulty all over the room talking about their fatigue, the bad weather and the mystery of the star. Perhaps someone could play 'We Three Kings' quietly on a recorder in the background while they travel.

Eventually the Wise Men could sit down in their first corner and sleep for a few moments. The group of Mary, Joseph and the baby is then illuminated again, waking the travellers, who stand, stumble towards them and fall on their knees to present their gifts.

The preparations will keep your children busy for several days beforehand. Crowns for the Wise Men can be made by cutting strips of cardboard (cereal packets are about the right thickness) 20″ long and 5″ wide. Draw a line to bisect each strip longways and cut points down to this on one side. Spray the crown with gold paint or cover it with silver foil and then decorate with anything pretty to give an impression of colourful richness – glitter, tinsel, strings of old beads, bright buttons, ribbons, sequins, even different coloured Smarties or fruit gums secured with a dab of glue or a blob of Plasticine. The ends can be overlapped so that they will fit any head and fastened together with paper clips or Sellotape. The crib can be made from a carrycot, doll's cot, drawer or cardboard box. Cover it with brown paper and fill with straw, hay, leaves or that shredded Cellophane which often comes around the Christmas turkey. The baby should be swaddled in muslin nappies or strips of old sheet to look authentic.

When the children arrive, explain what you are going to do and let them dress up. Lipstick, rouge and eyebrow pencil add to the fun and, of course false beards are essential. Those destined to play recorders or sing will probably want to dress up too, so have some cloaks, capes, old fur jackets for them to wear. Then rehearse the play for about an hour till everyone knows vaguely what he is supposed to be doing and when. Costumes off for tea – for which the traditional centrepiece is the Galette des Rois (p. 114), then draw the curtains, arrange the seating and lamps and dress up again.

Parents arrive to the strains of Christmas carols (on record or tape), are led into the darkened 'theatre' and conducted to their seats by ushers with torches. Pad out the play with several carols and recorder pieces and get the parents to swell the volume of the singing. The children will be filled with a sense of achievement at the end and will probably deserve a little parting present as they leave for home.

Easter Party (age ten upwards)

Long before it came to be the most important festival in the Christian calendar, Easter was the occasion for celebrating the arrival of spring – the sense of renewal and fertility and hope. The egg symbolized all this and the egg will inevitably dominate any Easter party.

Decorations should be essentially springlike. On the morning of the party, if you possibly can, make an Easter tree by cutting down a really large branch and anchoring it firmly in a heavy plant pot full of earth. Any branch which is just beginning to sprout young green leaves is beautiful, but if you know where to find catkins or pussy willows or if your garden boasts forsythia or a cherry tree then you have the makings of a memorable Easter tree. Once the branch is securely erected, decorate it with flowers, ribbons, beads, fluffy chickens, tiny sugar eggs. Criss-cross the tea table with sprays of leaves and ivy and put a posy of primroses, forget-me-nots or whatever is in flower at each place setting.

The weather is often surprisingly cold still and notoriously fickle, so this party will tend to be an indoor one although you can get your children to wrap tiny chocolate eggs in polythene (in case it rains on them), tie a thread around the polythene and loop them onto low branches of trees and bushes in the *back* garden (otherwise opportunists will cull them on their way to the front door) so that the guests can race around collecting them – in hats and coats if necessary – before leaving.

Invitations could go out on egg-shaped cards. The first

game should be a good ice breaker followed by a couple of strenuous games to work off surplus energy and excitement before they settle down to the serious business of egg decorating.

Before the guests arrive, hard-boil one egg for each of them with perhaps a few extra in reserve. In the days before the party your children will have been collecting a whole assortment of pretty tiny things – beads, buttons, feathers, sequins, lace, trimmings, bits of wool, cake decorations, coloured sticky paper. Put all these out on a table in saucers or little dishes, seat the children around with one tube of really good glue between two of them and a hard-boiled egg each. There should be a wide range of coloured felt pens available and egg cups or bits of egg boxes to support the eggs while they work on them. The variety of effects which can be achieved is amazing and you should allot prizes for the prettiest, the funniest, the most colourful, etc.

Then tea must, again, feature eggs. Stuffed eggs, egg cake, jelly eggs all go down well. Simnel cake – the traditional Easter cake in this country – is not usually very popular with children and, considering the price of ground almonds and dried fruit, this is really a blessing. But serve Easter biscuits, and try the Mocha cake, which is easy to make and always very much in demand; or anticipate May Day with a Maypole cake which is pretty and unusual (p. 96, 117 and 116). After tea a few quieter games before they leave, bearing their decorated eggs with them.

Garden Fête   (age eight upwards)

These are traditionally held in June, July or August but, if the weather is warm, there is no reason why they should not be held when the garden is fresh in May, or in September to distract attention from the back-to-school blues.

You will need the use of a garden, an area of grass or a leafy courtyard or school playground. It does not have to be very big as you can expand or contract your activities to fit the space.

Next consult with the children to decide on the cause you are going to support. Children are often anxious to help sick or handicapped children or there may be a children's or old people's home in the neighbourhood which appeals to their sense of community. Sometimes a local fund-raising effort to provide some amenity such as a swimming-pool or playing-fields is dear to their hearts and they welcome the chance to contribute.

Ask your children to go round their friends, to discover who would like to be involved, and then call a preliminary meeting to decide exactly who will do what – who will prepare and put up posters (and where and when), who will organize which stall and who will run which sideshow.

Here are some suggestions for stalls:

Secondhand jewellery – everybody has plenty if they search for it. Keep the prices low and all those odd bangles and beads will be snapped up as birthday presents for somebody's sister. Even the odd earrings can be attached to lengths of ribbon to make chokers or pendants.

Magazines and books – again, everybody has some, and at 1p or 2p each they will always sell.

Threepenny stall – can include anything at all which you want to sell for 3p.

Bottle stall – persuade as many people as you can to donate a bottle. It can be anything from vodka to vanilla essence. Buy a book of raffle tickets or cloakroom tickets, attach one number to each bottle and put its counterpart folded into a box adding a lot of numbered tickets for which there is no bottle. You then sell the tickets for 3p each and the lucky ones get the bottle with the corresponding number.

Home-made cakes and sweets – always a popular stall. Small individual cakes usually sell best to children as they are within the scope of their pocket money.

Refreshments – plastic cups of orange and lemon squash, home-made biscuits.

Flowers – which people contribute from their gardens.

Tiny buttonholes of fresh flowers wrapped around with foil and with a pin attached always sell well.

Suggestions for sideshows:

Puzzle boxes or Chinese laundry – *see* What To Play section under Ice Breakers.

Guessing–number of beans in a jar, weight of a cake, name of a doll, position of hidden treasure. Two pence a turn and you have to provide an acceptable prize.

Penny Dropping – have a bucket of water with a silver coin lying in the bottom at the centre and invite everybody to drop a 2p piece on top of it. If they succeed they take the silver coin but it is far more difficult than it sounds.

Darts contest – hang the board on a tree or wall in a safe corner, charge 2p a go and offer a small prize for the highest score.

Put up posters and do some private bullying among your friends and neighbours to persuade them to come along.

Get your own children to prepare a bran tub of tiny presents for all the helpers, which you keep hidden away until it is time to go home.

On the day itself ask the helpers to come round in the morning to rig up tables – tea chests, planks of wood between chairs – to cover them with bright cloths or curtains, to decorate them with ribbons, tinsel, little bells and flowers. Then they can arrange their goods, but keep any foodstuff indoors until the afternoon.

Try to have some music, as this makes it all seem gay and fun. You can have a radio outside – if this won't annoy the neighbours too much – or a record player or tape recorder by an open window.

About an hour and a half (say 2.30 till 4) is probably long enough for the actual fête and then your helpers will doubtless welcome some tea before clearing up. Save the bran tub of presents and the grand totalling of the proceeds until all is tidy again.

Midsummer Party (four to twelve)

The longest day of the year is 21 June, but Midsummer Day is actually 24 June. It is traditionally a day of magic when fairies feast and dance till dawn and people used to light great bonfires to encourage the sun to shine and ripen the harvest. Unfortunately it falls during the school term, but since this party is slightly mad anyway you can have it during any hot spell in the summer holidays and nobody will complain.

Cut invitations into flower shapes, or staple pressed or dried flowers to each one. Ask the guests to come with swim-suits and to wear funny hats – the madder the better.

The day before buy a gross of tiny paper bags and ask your children to peel about half a pound of potatoes for each guest and keep these in cold water overnight. Make an early start the next morning on cutting them into chips, pre-frying them and leaving them to drain on kitchen paper – it takes quite a long time and as the day gets hotter you won't particularly relish the operation.

Put up a table outside in the shade or in the garage, garden shed or porch and get out the hosepipe and as many plastic bowls, buckets and baby-baths as you can muster. The child-ren will get very wet so it is best to confine them strictly to the garden.

Judge the hats when the guests arrive and then, after they have changed into swimsuits, arrange some strenuous games (*see* p. 164). Once everyone is at boiling point put your eldest child in charge of hosing them down while you go and finish the chips. When you are ready ring a bell, sound a gong or blow a whistle and tell them to queue up at the open kitchen window. Slide a handful of chips into a bag for each child, insulate the bag with newspaper, and have a dustbin standing open near by into which they can toss their litter before rejoining the queue. They seem to love queueing up and having a good gossip while they wait their turn. Brace your-self for about four queue loads, after which the children will begin to lose interest and you strength. Close the window

firmly, put up a notice saying 'No More Frying' and divert
them to the table where there is a vast can of ice cream and
lots of little bowls containing *glacé* cherries, nuts, hundreds
and thousands, chocolate vermicelli, tiny biscuits, grapes,
etc., for them to concoct their own Knickerbocker Glories.

You can round off the afternoon with some quiet verbal
games. They will leave looking incredibly wet and greasy,
but they will have had a memorable time.

Camping Party (age six upwards)

Basically all you need for this is enough space to put up a tent
or two. If there isn't room in the garden, you may be able to
use a near-by field. You don't really need proper tents, but
nowadays many people do have a simple ridge tent which can
be easily erected, and this does lend authenticity. However,
young children in particular will enjoy a tent made by
draping a sheet, dust sheet or curtain over an old-fashioned
type of clothes-horse. Alternatively, if you have not got the
right sort of clothes-horse but do have a suitably placed tree,
tie a rope around its trunk, loop it over a low branch and
anchor it firmly to the ground at an angle from the tree. Then
throw over it an old cloth folded into a triangle and secure this
to the ground at intervals with tent pegs or metal meat
skewers. The only snag about these makeshift tents is that
they are not waterproof, so if the day turns to rain you will
either have to throw sheets of polythene over them or admit
defeat and move into the garage or garden shed.

Make it a lunch-time party for a change. This will give the
children time to shop for their own provisions and to clear up
the camp site at the end. It is more exciting and realistic if
you can build a brick surround to contain a small camp fire
but this will mean that you *must* be on hand throughout.

Welcome them at about 11.30 with a mug of fruit squash
while you plan the day and the menus together. Children
over eight may be allowed to do a bit of cooking on the fire.
Suggest baked beans as they are cheap, filling, popular, heat

up quickly and can be eaten from a bowl with a spoon. Things like sausages and potatoes in their skins take rather too long to cook properly, although you can cheat by starting these off in the oven. If the fire is hot enough, they can toast some bread to eat with the beans (those specially quick-toasting breads are most successful). Finish off with yogurt or fresh fruit and cheese. Once the menu is settled they can go off to the nearest shop for provisions with a budget provided by you.

Before lunch get the children to collect firewood and make gadgets for the camp – flagpole and flag, stand for washing up, twiggy branches to hang drying mugs and cloths upon, a spit to suspend the kettle over the fire.

Children who have already been to Scout and Guide camps are a great asset. As soon as lunch is ready, suggest that a kettle full of water is put on the fire to be heating for the washing up. (And as soon as the washing up is finished put another kettle on to make tea. It takes forever to come to the boil.)

After lunch play some restful pencil-and-paper games in the tents and then go on to more strenuous games while two or three of them have a go at making Campers' scones for tea. These are fairly crude but surprisingly good if eaten hot with butter and jam. Just throw two handfuls of flour into a bowl with two teaspoons of baking powder and add enough water to form a dough. Heat a small lump of butter in a frying pan over the camp fire. Mould the scones with the hands into little flat, round cakes about half an inch deep and cook them on both sides until brown.

Have tea at about 3 then there will be time for everyone to help with the clearing up before leaving at 4.

Hallowe'en Party (ages ten to twelve)

Hallowe'en is on 31 October. It is the eve of All Saints' Day, and popular mythology has attributed to it all sorts of mysterious happenings. The dead are reputed to rise from their graves and witches venture abroad to wreak havoc.

49

So a Hallowe'en party has to be very magical. Preparations should involve transforming the house into a cave of mystery – lights must be shrouded or hung with masks, or clear bulbs exchanged for red or green ones. Cut-out black cats, witches hats, bats and owls can proliferate and night lights inside jam jars on out-of-reach shelves give a pretty, flickering light. The traditional centrepiece is a pumpkin with the flesh scooped out (and made into jam or a pie) and eyes, mouth and nose cut out of the skin. A candle is fixed inside. If you can't obtain a pumpkin, make two or three smaller lanterns with turnips or swedes instead.

Food should be the sort that will look pretty by lantern light – stuffed tomatoes, stuffed eggs, polished red apples, frosted grapes, iced cakes decorated with silver balls.

There are several traditional games for Hallowe'en. One is apple bobbing. For this you place a large tub or baby bath full of water on the floor or on a low table. Put lots of thick layers of newspaper under and around it to soak up the overflow. Float some apples in the water and then the guests, with hands clasped behind their backs, are allowed four attempts each to try and catch an apple between their teeth. The one who catches the largest apple is supposed to be in line for the largest fortune! Have some man-size tissues or a towel at hand to dry wet faces.

Witch Hunt is another speciality but is not suitable for young children or the faint-hearted. It is too dangerous to reduce the house to *total* darkness but it should be almost completely dark. At the word 'Go' the witch runs away to hide and at the count of ten the other children call out, 'Where are you witch?' She answers with a ghostly cackle then slips away in the dark to another hiding place. Whoever catches the witch becomes the next witch.

You might have a session of magic before ending the party with a Treasure by Torchlight procession. Give each guest a torch – or ask them to bring their own – with coloured paper stuck over the end to add to the mystery. They set off round the garden, gloved and coated ready to leave, in a cautious crocodile, flashing torches to right and left. The treasure is concealed under plant pots all over the garden, with on top of each plant pot a little flag saying 'So-and-so's Treasure'.

Bonfire Party   (age three upwards)

There have been so many tragic accidents at family fireworks parties that they may well be ruled illegal in the next few years. Fireworks are pretty and exciting in a way that is unique, *but* they contain explosives, are very expensive and can be most alarming for young children, old people and pets. Even the inoffensive sparkler can be dangerous just after it has gone out, when the child is left in the dark with a red-hot wire precisely on the eye-level of other children. If, however, your children are passionately anxious to see some, get together with a few like-minded neighbouring parents and pool your resources. Resolve that the children will be kept behind some sort of barrier well out of the way with a couple of adults supervising them and that two other adults will be in charge of the covered box of fireworks and only they will set them up and let them off. No child must ever be allowed to put fireworks in his pockets.

The recurring nightmare is the one freaky firework which roars horizontally into the group of spectators, causing panic and sometimes disaster. There is no absolute guarantee against this happening, so, if you have qualms, and don't have big windows to watch through, settle for a simple Bonfire party, which can be fun and is much safer.

In the week or two before the party build a good, firm core for the fire in a safe spot well away from buildings and over-hanging trees. Once the foundation is made, the children can collect wood, cardboard, leaves and paper to add to the pile, but do show them how to pack it fairly tight and more or less vertical or you will find the fire doubled in circumference and thinly spread over half the garden. Keep the whole thing covered with a sheet of polythene, plastic, rubber or canvas.

51

The children can also prepare a guy. The body might be made out of an old sack, pillow-case or strong paper bag, and the head can be made from an old pair of tights. Stuff the tights with dry leaves, straw or hay then draw them together at the waistband to form the top of the head. Now bunch them up and tie a string around the top of the legs to form the neck. The stuffed tight legs will go right down inside the torso to hold the head firm. Thread a stick through the top of the sack, pillow-case or paper bag to form the arms then have somebody suspend the stuffed tights inside the body while it is filled with twigs, leaves, balls of crumpled newspaper and packed tight. Sew roughly across the shoulders of the sack with string or thread and make a mask from a circle of cardboard which can be glued or tacked onto the head. Finishing touches can be any old hats, scarves, broken pipes, ancient cardigans, jackets, trousers, gloves.

The guy can be propped in the porch to greet the guests who should be invited for about five o'clock (with torches, since it gets dark early at that time of year). Don't let them into the house; instead set them off straight away in a torch-light procession, bearing the guy either seated on an old chair which you want to burn or in a big cardboard box, or carried unceremoniously by his arms to his hot seat on top of the bonfire. The procession has more panache if accompanied by some children on mouth organs, accordions, drums or whistles.

Before actually lighting the fire you could play follow-my-leader or tag in the dark with torches bobbing everywhere. Then, when the children are well warmed up, make them stand right back while you set the fire alight. If you have a good hard centre of old planks and chunks of wood, it will burn for some time and you can have a sing-song while you watch. In these days of central heating and gas and electric fires, the living flame has a great fascination for children and they will happily watch it until it burns right down; but because they are not familiar with the nature of fire watch carefully that they do not do anything silly or dangerous.

Then back to the house and the bonfire supper which you

have left laid out on a big table covered with a bright cloth and lit with night lights and safe, squat candles. Lots of hot soup and potatoes in their jackets to start with followed by an assortment of things that will look pretty by candlelight – a pyramid of polished rosy apples, little cakes spangled with silver balls, orange halves filled with jelly.

You could finish the meal with a couple of boxes of indoor fireworks, which are harmless enough providing you protect your table. Then a few games before the guests go home at about 7.

Carol Party (age nine upwards)

Carol parties are very little trouble to prepare or run and the children always enjoy them and feel they have achieved something.

Decide first what charity you want to support. The personal columns of national and local newspapers will give your children some ideas and addresses, and most charities will send you official collecting tins and sometimes carol sheets as well.

Send out invitations for about 5.30 p.m. (so that householders will be back from work), advising the guests to wear warm and waterproof clothing. Or, if you want to hold an earlier party, consider carol singing in a group in a traffic-free shopping centre, outside the local library or railway or bus station, or at any other focal point in the area.

Prepare lanterns by fixing candles onto the bases of old jam jars with Plasticine, cutting fancy shades from coloured paper, tying string around the tops of the jars and then securing them to poles. These are quite safe, look pretty and give enough light to read the words on the carol sheet. If you prefer to use torches, ask each child to bring one if he can and cover the bulb end with coloured paper or cloth before you set off.

You or some other adult should accompany the children, to bring them back if they begin to freeze or flag, to prevent them running across roads in their excitement, or in case, as sometimes happens, any householder is disagreeable to them. Make a short tour of neighbouring houses singing a couple of carols at each then ringing the bell and politely explaining your mission. When the collecting tins make a good healthy rattle, back home to a supper starting with hot soup and with a treasure-packed Gingerbread House as the centrepiece (p. 115).

Depending on the time, you may then round off the evening with magic or a few quiet games. The children are always pleased to receive an official letter of thanks and a receipt for the amount collected when you return the collecting tins.

Christmas Concert   (ages four to ten)

Most children's libraries put up beautiful big Christmas trees in the week or so before Christmas, and many hold concerts around it consisting of carols, poems, short seasonal stories and a few children playing violins, recorders, guitars or flutes. If your local library or community centre does not do this, it is well worth suggesting it.

It is encouraging for the organizers if you undertake to bring along a group of children. Your own contribution to the occasion will depend on what time the concert is scheduled to take place – you could have tea before or after. Since the children will be required to sit still for some time at the concert, include some fairly strenuous games to work off surplus energy.

Boxing Day Party   (age four upwards)

It sounds appalling even to contemplate a children's party the day after Christmas, but there are a number of built-in advantages: it tends otherwise to be a day of anti-climax and thus bad temper; there are lots of odds and ends of food around; it is often a lovely day of cold, clear sunlight.

54

Leave the adults in peace and sweep the children off for a brisk winter walk. It's a great day for meets and you may be lucky enough to see the huntsmen in their scarlet coats streaming across the fields. The children can collect any pretty stones, mosses, fir cones, small pieces of evergreen or berries that they find, so that when you return they can make a winter garden. An old tin tray covered with sand or soil makes a suitable base and a piece of mirror serves as a frozen lake. An aerosol of sparkly snow and a few tiny figures or animals or little model buildings will finish off the scene.

Tea on Boxing Day is a good time for an open-sandwich competition. Put out little pots containing all the Christmas leftovers – olives, gherkins, capers, shrimps, grapes, cheese, tomatoes, cold chipolatas, nuts and anything else there is. Each child has a plate with three buttered savoury biscuits and three thin rounds of French bread or three buttered bridge rolls. Using these as a base, they set to work concocting mouth-watering open sandwiches. It is a fiddly business and takes ages, but when they have finally completed them you should judge them for prettiness and gastronomic harmony before letting them tuck in. (For some reason they always eat each other's!) Appetites will probably be a little fragile after the excesses of Christmas, so the rest of the fare should be the sort that will not take long to prepare and can be used up if they don't eat it all – cubes of pineapple wrapped in ham, short lengths of celery stuffed with cheese or turkey, savoury and sweet biscuits and fresh fruit.

Finish up with a few quiet games which will not alienate dozing grandparents and visiting aunties and you will find that a day which can be somewhat trying has passed happily.

WHAT TO EAT

The parties which leave glittering memories are not only those which are fun but those where the food is something special. Children are gastronomically more sophisticated and adventurous than ever before, and even if dishes are new to them, they will try them if they are appetizingly presented.

Many children love to cook and help in the preparations for a party. The recipes which are starred (*) are quite straightforward and foolproof and can safely be entrusted to almost any child over the age of seven.

Each recipe will feed about six children.

3. SOUPS

These home-made soups are inexpensive, nourishing and always popular in small servings. I have not included here the rich meaty soups which really constitute a meal for a small tummy because, excellent as they can be, they are troublesome and often costly to prepare. Iced soups are new to many children but served in a small glass dish with a couple of ice cubes and garnished with a sprig of mint or chopped parsley they make an attractive start to a summer-time party meal. Hot soups are lovely to come home to after some outdoor activity in cold weather. They can be ladled into mugs (if smooth) or served in individual earthenware pots (if chunky) and topped with fried bread initials, grated cheese or chopped herbs.

Because of the large quantities of hot liquid involved most of the recipes are unsuitable for children to make, although two are made from only cold ingredients. But soup can always be prepared well in advance and then reheated.

Iced Soups

Iced Beetroot Soup

Frosty pink, an exciting start to the meal.

¾ lb beetroot
1½ pints salted water
vinegar
2 eggs
seasoning

Peel and chop the beetroot. Cook it in the water with a little vinegar added for 20 minutes. Sieve. Beat up the eggs and stir them in. Re-heat, stirring all the time, then season and sieve again. Cool and chill thoroughly.

Iced Cucumber Soup

An economical soup with a fresh, minty flavour.

1½ pints chicken stock
1 small onion
1 cucumber
1 sprig mint
1 level dessertspoon arrowroot
a little milk
1 tablespoon cream (or top of the milk)

Add the chopped onion to the chicken stock, bring to the boil, cover and simmer for 10 to 15 minutes. Peel the cucumber, chop it small and add it to the stock together with the mint. Cook until tender (10 to 15 minutes). Pass through a sieve or liquidizer and return to the pan. Blend the arrowroot with a little milk and mix it in. Bring to the boil, stirring all the time, and cook for half a minute. Add seasoning and cream. Turn into a bowl and chill. Serve topped with thinly sliced cucumber and sprigs of mint.

Iced Pickled Cucumber Soup

½ lb pickled cucumbers
2 pints beef stock
2 lumps sugar
¼ pint cream
mace, ginger, allspice, pepper and salt

Chop the cucumbers and simmer for 30 minutes in the stock. Sieve. Add the sugar and a pinch of mace, ground ginger, allspice, pepper and salt. Heat the cream separately and stir it in. Cool, chill and serve garnished with chopped mint.

Children's Gazpacho*

½ cucumber
6 oz tomatoes
1 medium onion
1 medium green pepper
3 oz crustless bread
2 cloves garlic
1 tablespoon mayonnaise
1 teaspoon paprika
1½ teaspoons salt
2 pints water
4 tablespoons vinegar

Peel the cucumber, tomatoes and onion and chop roughly with the flesh of the green pepper and the bread. Peel and crush the garlic and mix everything together. Sieve and chill thoroughly and garnish with chopped parsley before serving.

Iced Green Soup*

You simply liquidize the following ingredients, season and chill.

63

5 oz spinach
½ peeled cucumber
juice of 1 lemon
1 pint water
1 oz watercress
2 sliced spring onions
½ apple
3 sprigs mint

Iced Cream of Mushroom Soup

1¼ oz butter
1½ oz flour
1½ pints chicken stock
6 oz mushrooms
½ pint single cream
tarragon leaves

Melt the butter over gentle heat, stir in the flour, pour on the stock and bring to the boil. Rinse and slice the mushrooms and stir into the soup with the cream. Simmer for 5 minutes, then sieve and leave to cool, whisking occasionally. Chill. Whisk again before serving and garnish with a dusting of chopped tarragon leaves.

Iced Shrimp Soup

1 pint cooked shrimps (in their shells)
3 tablespoons fresh white breadcrumbs
juice of ½ lemon
nutmeg
1 egg yolk
¼ pint cream or milk
seasoning
Stock:
½ lb cod, haddock or any white fish
the shrimp shells
1 onion
herbs
peel of ½ lemon
1½ pints water

Make the stock by simmering the fish, the shrimp shells, the onion, herbs and peel of the lemon together in 1½ pints of water for about 20 minutes. Strain (give the white fish to the cat or keep it for fishcakes) and add the breadcrumbs. Reserve a few shrimps for garnishing and pound the rest with the juice of the lemon and a pinch of nutmeg. Gradually add the stock. Heat in a pan for 5 minutes then press through a sieve. Beat the yolk and the cream or milk together. Stir in 3 table-spoons of the hot soup and return to the pan. Stir until the soup is hot but do not let it boil. Season, cool and chill thoroughly. When serving garnish each bowl with the shrimps you have kept back, a little chopped, peeled cucumber and a slice of lemon.

Iced Tomato Soup

A little orange flavour gives this soup unusual subtlety.

2 lb tomatoes
1 small onion
bay leaf
6 peppercorns
2 cloves
1 lemon
2 pints chicken or vegetable stock
1 orange
1 level tablespoon arrowroot
3 tablespoons cream
seasoning

Wash the tomatoes, cut in half, squeeze gently to remove the seeds and discard them. Put the tomatoes into a saucepan with the peeled and quartered onion, the bay leaf, pepper-corns, cloves, a strip of lemon peel and the stock. Cover and simmer for 1 hour. Sieve. Mix the arrowroot with 3 table-spoons water, add to the pan and bring back to the boil. Season and stir in a little of the juice of the lemon. Cool and chill. Serve with a spoonful of cream in each bowl and sprinkle with grated orange rind.

Vichyssoise

4 leeks
1 medium onion
2 oz butter
5 medium potatoes
1¾ pints chicken stock
1 tablespoon salt
¼ pint cream or top of the milk
chives

Finely slice the onion and the white part of the leeks and brown them slightly in the butter. Add the thinly sliced potatoes, the stock and salt and simmer for about 40 minutes. Strain and sieve. When cold stir in the cream and chill thoroughly. Sprinkle with chopped chives before serving.

Hot Soups

Cauliflower Soup

1 medium cauliflower
1½ pints stock
1 onion
mixed herbs
seasoning
2 egg yolks
3 tablespoons cream
3 tablespoons milk

Divide the cauliflower into small sprigs, rinse and put into a saucepan with the stock, herbs, onion and seasoning. Cover and cook for 30 to 40 minutes then sieve. Let it cool and then stir in the egg yolks, cream and milk. Cook without boiling until the soup thickens slightly.

Celery Soup

1 lb celery
1 oz margarine
1 small onion

1 pint stock or water
½ oz cornflour
¼ pint milk
seasoning

Clean the celery thoroughly and chop it roughly. Melt the margarine in a saucepan and toss the celery and chopped onion in it for a few minutes. Add the stock, season, bring to the boil, cover and simmer for about 15 minutes. Sieve and then stir in the cornflour mixed to a smooth cream with the milk. Stir until boiling and cook for 2 minutes.

Chestnut Soup

A lovely soup to make when chestnuts are cheap or if you discover some growing wild in the woods.

1½ pints beef stock
¾ lb chestnuts
1 heaped teaspoon cornflour
¼ pint milk
½ oz margarine
seasoning

The chestnuts must first be skinned and there are two ways of doing this. First score the outside with a small, sharp knife or nick it with scissors then either put them in a baking tin in a low oven for 20 minutes or drop them into boiling water and boil for 20 minutes. Remove the shells and brown skin and chop the chestnuts roughly. Place them in a saucepan with the stock and seasoning and simmer gently until they become pulpy. Sieve. Mix the cornflour smoothly with the milk, add to the soup and return to the pan. Stir until boiling. Add the margarine in tiny pieces, cook for 2 minutes, season again and serve with diced fried bread.

Chicken Soup

Children always seem to like this.

1 oz butter
1 oz flour

¾ *pint chicken stock*
¾ *pint milk*
nutmeg
seasoning
6 oz chopped cooked chicken
2 tablespoons cream

Melt the butter in a saucepan, stir in the flour and cook gently for 3 minutes. Gradually add the stock and then the milk, stirring. Bring to the boil and season. Toss in the chopped chicken and cook gently for 10 to 15 minutes. Stir in the cream and serve.

Leek Soup

3 large leeks
1 oz butter
1 chopped onion
1½ pints beef stock
1 bay leaf
3 cloves
2 large potatoes
seasoning

Clean the leeks and slice them finely. Heat the butter in a large saucepan and sauté the leeks and onion for 10 minutes. Add the stock, bay leaf, cloves and potatoes cut into small cubes and season well. Cover the pan and cook gently for 20 minutes.

Lentil Soup

Lentils are a much neglected source of vegetable protein in this country. A very heartening soup.

¼ *pint orange lentils*
1 onion
1 carrot
2 sticks celery
½ *oz margarine*
mixed herbs

seasoning
1 pint stock
½ pint milk
½ oz flour
little single cream

Wash the lentils and cover with boiling water. Peel and chop the onion and carrot and chop the celery. Heat the margarine in a heavy saucepan and sauté the vegetables lightly for about 10 minutes. Add the seasoning and herbs. Pour in the stock, bring to the boil and add the drained and rinsed lentils. Simmer for about 1½ hours then sieve. Re-heat the lentil purée with ¼ pint of the milk and mix the flour to a smooth paste with the rest of it. Stir this into the soup just before it reaches boiling point again. Boil for 5 minutes, stirring, and add a little cream before serving.

If preferred, this soup may be served with Ham Balls made by mixing together 1 cup of minced ham or boiled bacon, 1 tablespoon of flour, 1 egg and seasoning. Form into very small balls and simmer in the soup for 10 minutes.

Lettuce Soup

A fresh soup useful when you have a glut of lettuces in the garden.

2 lettuces
handful spinach
handful parsley
2 oz butter
seasoning
1½ pints stock
1 egg yolk

Cut the lettuces and spinach into strips and cook them in the butter together with the chopped parsley until they are quite soft. Add the stock and seasoning. Bring to the boil and simmer for 45 minutes. Discard any hard or stringy bits and beat in the egg yolk just before serving.

Mushroom Soup

½ lb mushrooms
1 oz margarine
1 small onion
1 pint milk and stock or milk and water
seasoning
mixed herbs
½ oz flour
2 egg yolks
¼ pint cream

Rinse and slice the mushrooms. Melt the margarine in a saucepan and fry the onion and mushrooms in it lightly. Add the milk and stock, seasoning and mixed herbs, cover and cook gently for about 30 minutes. Sieve. Place the flour in the rinsed saucepan and beat in the soup gradually over gentle heat. Stir until boiling, then cool. Beat up the egg yolks with the cream and strain into the cooled soup then re-heat until it thickens. Serve sprinkled with chopped parsley.

Onion Soup

Good for a winter party.

1 lb onions
1 stick celery
½ oz margarine
½ oz cornflour
1 pint stock or water
½ pint milk
seasoning

Peel the onions and chop them roughly with the celery. Melt the margarine in a saucepan and sauté the vegetables in it for a few minutes. When the fat has been absorbed add the stock and seasoning, bring to the boil, cover and simmer until tender (approximately 15 minutes). Sieve. Mix the cornflour smoothly with the milk and add. Return to the pan, stir until boiling and cook for 2 minutes. Serve with tiny cubes of fried bread.

Parsley Soup

Rich in Vitamin C and a useful soup when you have loads of parsley in the garden and not much else.

4½ oz parsley
2 medium onions
2 oz butter or margarine
2 medium potatoes
seasoning
½ teaspoon sugar
½ pint water
1½ pints milk
1 egg yolk

Chop the onion quite small and cook it in the butter or margarine until transparent. Roughly chop the parsley and add it together with the peeled and quartered potatoes. Season, add the sugar and cook slowly with the water in a covered pan until the vegetables are soft. Sieve, and add the milk. At the last minute stir in the beaten egg yolk and garnish with chopped parsley.

Pea Soup

Cooking the pea pods in the stock adds flavour and colour to this soup.

2 lb fresh peas (in pods)
2 pints chicken stock
1 bay leaf
1 teaspoon salt
2 oz butter or margarine
4 teaspoons flour
¼ pint cream

Shell the peas. Wash the pods and put them into a large saucepan with the stock, bay leaf and salt. Cover and cook for 40 minutes then strain and discard the pods. Pour the liquid back into the pan, add the peas and simmer for 10 minutes. Sieve. Melt the butter or margarine in the pan, stir in the flour and soup and re-heat, then stir in the cream.

Pumpkin Soup

To use up the flesh of the Hallowe'en lanterns.

2 lb pumpkin flesh
seasoning
1 stick celery
1½ pints milk
1 pint stock
4 oz prawns or shrimps (optional)

Cut the pumpkin flesh into small pieces. Season them and put them into a thick saucepan with the chopped celery. Cover with the milk and the stock and simmer for about 30 minutes. Sieve, and add the chopped prawns or shrimps if desired. Stir in a good lump of butter just before serving.

Tomato Soup with Orange

The flavour of this soup is enhanced by rubbing a sugar lump over the rind of an orange to absorb the zest.

1 lb tomatoes – fresh or tinned
1 small carrot
1 small onion
1 bay leaf
strip lemon peel
3 peppercorns
1½ pints chicken stock
salt
1½ oz margarine
1½ oz flour
1 lump of sugar and a little granulated sugar
¼ pint thin cream
1 orange

Wash the tomatoes, cut them in half, squeeze to remove the seeds and discard them. Slice the onion and carrot and put them in a saucepan, with the tomatoes, bay leaf, lemon rind, peppercorns and stock. Season, cover and simmer for 1 hour. Sieve. Rinse out the pan and melt the margarine in it then stir in the flour and add the tomato liquid. Rub the lump of sugar over the outside of the orange and add to the soup plus a little extra sugar. Simmer for 5 minutes. Add the cream gradually and serve.

Watercress Soup

2 bunches watercress (approximately ½ lb)
½ oz butter
1 pint stock
seasoning
1 tablespoon cornflour
¼ pint milk
2 to 3 tablespoons cream

Wash the watercress and remove the coarse stalks. Melt the butter in a saucepan, add the watercress (reserving a few sprigs) and toss over very gentle heat for 2 to 3 minutes. Add the stock and seasoning, cover and simmer gently for 20 to 30 minutes. Sieve, return to the pan and add the cornflour blended with the milk. Bring to the boil, stirring, and cook for 5 to 8 minutes. Adjust the seasoning, stir in the cream and garnish with watercress.

Fried Bread Initials

Cut the children's initials out of rather stale, thickish bread with a small, sharp knife and fry quickly in deep fat until crisp and golden. Drain and keep crisp in an airtight tin, then float on top of each child's bowl of soup.

4. SAVOURIES

Savoury things are increasingly popular at children's parties. These are tasty, look appetizing and are inexpensive to make.

Apple Sausage Roll*

A good, hearty dish to serve hot for a winter lunch-time party or cold for a picnic or summer tea.

1 lb beef sausage meat
3 cooking apples
1 onion
3 oz fresh breadcrumbs
1 egg
seasoning

Roll out the sausage meat on greaseproof paper into a rectangle ½" thick. Mix together the diced cooking apples, chopped onion, breadcrumbs and egg. Season, spread over the sausage meat and roll it up. Place in a buttered baking dish on the centre shelf of a moderate oven (Reg. 4, 355 °F.) for 45 minutes. Sprinkle with dried breadcrumbs and chopped parsley.

Bacon Rolls*

6 long rashers of streaky bacon
2 onions
4 tablespoons rolled oats
a little chopped sage
2 oz chopped suet
milk to bind
1 oz margarine
seasoning

Remove the rind from the bacon and cut each rasher in half. Grate the onions or chop them finely and mix with the oats, sage, seasoning and suet. Bind together with the milk. Divide this stuffing into twelve and roll half a rasher around each piece. Pack closely in a greased fireproof dish, dot with margarine and bake in a fairly hot oven (Reg. 6, 400 °F.) for 15 minutes.

Cheese Aigrettes

These are invaluable. They are cheap to make, can be prepared in advance, stored in an airtight tin and quickly heated through in the oven or frying pan. They may be eaten in the (greasy) fingers or speared with toothpicks and there are *never* any left.

¼ pint water
2 oz grated cheese
2½ oz flour
2 eggs
1 oz margarine
seasoning

Boil the water and margarine together. Add the flour and beat until smooth then add the eggs by degrees. Beat thoroughly to incorporate lots of air and stir in the cheese and seasoning. Heat some deep fat until it is slightly smoking and drop in small teaspoonsfuls of the mixture. Let them cook for about 10 minutes until crisp and golden. Drain on kitchen paper.

Cheese and Bacon Cakes*

4 oz flour
2 oz semolina
4 level teaspoons baking powder
½ level teaspoon salt
½ level teapoon mustard powder
2 oz margarine
2 oz finely grated cheese
4 rashers crisply fried bacon
2 eggs
2 tablespoons milk

Sift the flour with the semolina, baking powder, salt and mustard and rub in the margarine. Add the grated cheese and crumbled bacon and stir in the beaten eggs and milk. Spoon into well greased patty tins and bake in a hot oven (Reg. 6, 400 °F.) for about 20 minutes until well risen and firm to the touch. Best served hot with butter and watercress.

Cheese and Onion Cakes*

8 oz flour
2 teaspoons baking powder
½ teaspoon salt
2 oz butter or margarine
4 oz grated cheese
½ pint milk (approximately)
3 oz finely chopped onion
dripping

Sift the flour with the baking powder and salt. Rub in the butter or margarine, add the cheese and stir in enough milk to make a soft dough. Turn onto a floured board and knead lightly then roll out to a thickness of ½″. Cut into 2″ rounds and bake in a hot oven (Reg. 6, 400 °F.) for about 15 minutes. Split and sandwich together with the onions lightly fried in dripping.

Cheese Scotch Eggs

A change from the usual version made with sausage meat.

6 hard-boiled eggs
8 oz grated cheese
2 oz flour
1 teaspoon salt
1 teaspoon Worcester sauce
1 egg
2 tablespoons milk
deep fat to fry
dried breadcrumbs

Mix the cheese, flour and seasoning together. Add the egg and milk and beat well. Shell the eggs and, with wet hands, coat them with the cheese mixture. Roll in the dried breadcrumbs and fry in deep fat for about 3 minutes. Drain, cool slightly and cut across in half.

Egg Cake

6 eggs
salad cream
chopped herbs

Keeping the yolks intact break the eggs into a buttered fireproof dish just large enough to hold them rather crowdedly. Stand the dish in a baking tin of boiling water and cook in a moderate oven (Reg. 4, 355 °F.) for about 10 minutes until the eggs are set. Leave to cool and then turn onto a dish and coat carefully with salad cream into which you have stirred some finely chopped herbs.

Eggs – stuffed*

6 eggs
1 oz grated cheese
seasoning
a little salad cream
parsley

Hard boil the eggs, cut in half and scoop out the yolks. Cut a tiny slice off the base of each white so that they will stand firmly. Mash up the yolks with the cheese, chopped parsley and seasoning. Bind together with the salad cream and pile back into the whites.

French Twists*

For the more sophisticated who like the taste of olives. Make the day before.

1 French loaf
4 tomatoes
1 onion
2 tablespoons capers
1 green pepper
2 oz black olives
2 oz green olives
2 oz gherkins
a little olive oil
seasoning

Cut the loaf in half lengthwise and scoop out the crumbs into a bowl. Stir in the finely chopped tomatoes, onion, capers, green pepper, stoned olives, gherkins and seasoning and work it together with a little olive oil so that it binds. Fill the loaf, press the halves well together, wrap it in foil and chill overnight. Slice thinly and serve.

Ham Loaves

Delicious hot or cold.

1 lb potatoes
6 oz ham
1 oz butter
2 eggs
seasoning
nutmeg

Boil the potatoes, mash them and mix in the finely chopped ham, the butter, eggs, seasoning and nutmeg. Mould the mixture into little rolls and fry them or bake them in a slow oven (Reg. 2, 310 °F.) for 30 minutes.

Ham Mousse

It is often possible to buy trimmings of ham at a much reduced price and these are ideal for ham mousse.

¾ lb cooked ham
approximately 1 tablespoon wine or sherry
3 oz cream
nutmeg
pepper
3 egg whites

Mince the ham, stir in the wine or sherry, season and add the cream. Beat the whites of egg to a stiff froth and stir them in lightly. Turn into a fireproof dish, cover with foil, stand in a baking tin of hot water and cook in a moderate oven (Reg. 4, 355 °F.) for about 30 minutes. May be served hot or cold.

Ham Ramekins

Odds and ends of ham are also ideal for these ramekins. They can be prepared in advance up to the point where the meringue is added.

4 oz finely chopped cooked ham
2 eggs
4 tablespoons milk
1 teaspoon chopped mixed herbs
½ teaspoon mustard
seasoning

Separate the yolks from the whites of the eggs. Beat the yolks slightly and add the ham, milk, herbs, mustard and seasoning. Place in individual fireproof china or foil dishes (the sort in which little pies are often packaged will do quite well) and bake in a moderate oven (Reg. 4, 355 °F.) until set (approximately 15 minutes). Beat the whites of egg to a stiff froth, season and pile roughly above the level of the dishes. Return to the oven and bake again until the white of egg is crisp and lightly browned (about another 15 minutes). Serve hot.

Kedgeree

Improbable as it may sound, I always find this is very much in demand. It can be made beforehand and heated through with a little extra butter. It goes a long way and is not expensive.

1 lb smoked haddock or smoked cod
½ lb long grain rice
2 hard-boiled eggs
2 oz butter or margarine
seasoning
parsley

Boil the fish and flake it. Boil the rice until tender. Chop the hard-boiled eggs. Melt the butter or margarine in a saucepan and add the fish, rice, seasoning and eggs. Stir around until thoroughly hot and serve strewn with parsley.

Kipper Pâté

Excellent with thin toast, brown bread or plain biscuits.

6 kipper fillets
½ pint white sauce
2 hard-boiled eggs
pepper
mixed herbs
1 clove garlic
2 bay leaves

Poach the kipper fillets and let them cool. Chop and mix with the sauce, chopped eggs, crushed garlic, herbs and pepper. Lay the bay leaves in a buttered fireproof dish and pile in the kipper mixture. Smooth it down, cover and cook for 30 minutes in a moderate oven (Reg. 4, 355 °F.).

Meat – potted*

We used to be able to buy little earthenware pots of home-made potted meat sealed with clarified butter from grocers' shops. It is an excellent traditional way of using up left-over meat and deserves to be revived.

approximately ½ lb cooked meat (beef, veal, pork, lamb, etc.)
2 oz cooked ham or bacon
nutmeg
seasoning
2 oz softened butter

Finely mince the meat and the ham or bacon. Add the seasoning and beat in the butter gradually. Put into small pots or jars and pour a little melted butter on top. Keep in refrigerator.

Meatballs

A clever way to make a small quantity of inexpensive meat go a very long way.

¾ lb beef sausage meat
1 egg
1 clove garlic, crushed
seasoning
1 grated onion
1 cup fresh breadcrumbs
dried breadcrumbs

Mix all the ingredients except the dried crumbs together and form into balls the size of a walnut. Roll in dried crumbs and fry in shallow fat then cover and finish off in a low oven for 30 minutes.

Meat Loaf

One of the simplest of recipes and yet it tastes delicious and is a great favourite cold with salad, on toast or biscuits or in sandwiches.

1 lb raw minced beef
¼ lb fresh breadcrumbs
2 oz minced bacon
1 egg
dried breadcrumbs

Mix the first four ingredients together and form into a roll. Wrap in foil or tie in a cloth and place in slowly boiling water in a covered pan for 2 hours, or pack into a 2 lb bread tin, cover with foil and stand in a roasting tin half full of water in a low oven (Reg. 3, 330 °F.) for 2 hours. Roll in fried, dried breadcrumbs and leave to cool.

Mushrooms – stuffed*

These can be prepared well in advance and cooked in the last half hour.

12 medium mushrooms
2 dessertspoons chopped cooked ham or bacon
2 teaspoons chopped parsley
2 tablespoons fresh breadcrumbs
1 dessertspoon finely chopped onion
1 oz margarine
seasoning
2 tablespoons top of the milk
3 large tomatoes
12 squares of fried bread (to stand mushrooms on)

Rinse the mushrooms, peel them and remove the stalks. Chop the stalks finely. Melt the margarine and fry the onion in it slightly before stirring in the ham, parsley, crumbs, stalks, seasoning and milk. Beat over gentle heat for a minute to bind them together. Grease a baking sheet, stand the mushroom caps upside down upon it and fill with the mixture. Cover with greased paper and bake in a moderate (Reg. 4, 355 °F.) oven for 20 minutes. Serve them on a square of fried bread with a slice of tomato on it.

Potato Cakes

Very good sandwiched together with chopped bacon or fried onions.

1½ lb mashed potato
3 tablespoons flour
fat to fry
seasoning

Mix the potatoes with flour and seasoning. Roll out on a floured board to about ¼″ thickness. Cut into rounds and fry in a little hot fat until lightly browned on both sides. Serve hot.

Potatoes – stuffed*

6 medium-sized potatoes
2 tablespoons milk
3 oz grated cheese
1 oz butter or margarine
seasoning
parsley

Scrub the potatoes and bake them in their skins in a hot oven (Reg. 6, 400 °F.) for about 1 hour. Cut away a portion from the flat side of each, scoop out the potato and sieve it. Put it into a saucepan with the other ingredients but keep back a tablespoon of the cheese. Beat over gentle heat until creamy then pile back into the potato cases. Sprinkle with the rest of the cheese and brown under the grill. Brush with melted margarine and sprinkle with parsley.

Quiche

This is marvellous for picnics and a great stand-by for all manner of parties. Make it in a fluted flan dish about 8″ in diameter.

baked short crust case
4 oz bacon
4 tablespoons milk
2 eggs
pepper
4 oz grated cheese

Cut the bacon into small pieces, fry them lightly and place in the pastry case. Heat the milk and pour it onto the beaten eggs. Season and pour over the bacon. Sprinkle the cheese on top and bake in a cool oven (Reg. 3, 330 °F.) for about 30 minutes until golden and set. Garnish with watercress or parsley and serve hot or cold.

Sardine Rolls

8 oz short crust pastry
1 can sardines
pepper
vinegar
3 oz grated cheese
1 egg

Mash the sardines with the pepper and vinegar. Roll out the pastry thinly and cut into rectangles. Sprinkle with cheese and place some of the filling on each. Brush the long edges with beaten egg and roll up. Brush over with a little more beaten egg, place on a greased baking sheet and bake in a hot oven (Reg. 6, 400 °F.) for 15 minutes.

Tomatoes – stuffed*

6 large tomatoes
3 slices white bread
1 clove garlic
olive oil
2 tablespoons chopped parsley
seasoning

Cut the tomatoes in half, squeeze gently to remove the seeds and discard them. Invert the tomatoes on a plate to drain. Rub the bread with the cut garlic clove, crumble it and sprinkle well with olive oil, then mix with the chopped parsley and season well. Fill the tomato halves with the mixture and bake in a moderate oven (Reg. 4, 355 °F.) for about 15 minutes.

5. BISCUITS

I have included quite a lot of biscuit recipes, as home-made biscuits are economical, easy and quick for children to make and a pleasant change from the predictable packaged product.

Savoury Biscuits

Almond Sablés

6 oz flour
4 oz margarine
1½ oz ground almonds

3 oz grated cheese
seasoning
1 yolk
1 tablespoon water
1 beaten egg for gilding
Filling:
1 teaspoon arrowroot or cornflour
1 egg
1 level teaspoon paprika
seasoning
¼ pint warm milk
1½ oz grated cheese

Sift the flour and rub in the margarine. Mix in the almonds, cheese and seasoning. Beat the yolk with half the water. Add to the mixture and work up to a firm paste adding more water if necessary. Roll out to about ⅛″ thick and stamp into small rounds (approximately 1½″ in diameter). Brush half of them with the beaten egg and bake them all in a moderate oven (Reg. 4, 355 °F.) for about 15 minutes until pale golden brown. Cool slightly before removing from tray. To make the filling: mix the arrowroot or cornflour with the egg yolk and seasoning. Pour on the milk and stir until boiling. Remove from the heat and add the cheese. Whip the egg white stiffly and fold lightly into the mixture. Re-heat carefully to cook the white but do not let it boil. Put a tea-spoonful of the filling on each biscuit which has not been painted with egg and cover lightly with the gilded halves. Serve hot.

Anchovy Biscuits*
Many children like the salty, astringent taste of these.

6 oz flour
3 oz margarine
1 egg
1 teaspoon anchovy essence
pepper

Filling:

8 anchovy fillets
2 hard-boiled egg yolks
2 dessertspoons margarine (melted)
6 tablespoons double cream

Rub the margarine into the flour, add the egg, anchovy essence and enough water to make a stiff paste. Roll out thinly, stamp into small rounds and bake in a moderate oven (Reg. 4, 355 °F.) for about 15 minutes.

To make the filling: pound the anchovy fillets and mix them together with the egg yolks, melted margarine and pepper. Sieve. Whip the cream stiffly and stir lightly into the anchovy mixture. With a forcing bag or teaspoon place some in the centre of each biscuit.

Pretzels*

Caraway seeds went out of fashion for so long that they are now an interesting new taste experience for most children.

4 oz flour
2 oz margarine
1 oz sugar
2 teaspoons caraway seeds
1 egg

Rub the fat into the flour and mix in the sugar and caraway seeds. Add sufficient egg to bind into a stiff paste. Divide into 12 pieces. Roll each piece into a cylinder in the palm of the hand and tie into a knot. Place on a greased baking sheet, brush with beaten egg and bake in a moderate oven (Reg. 4, 355 °F.) for 15 to 20 minutes.

Cheese Biscuits*

4 oz flour
4 oz butter or margarine
4 oz grated cheese
seasoning
1 egg

Sift the flour and rub in the butter or margarine. Add the cheese and seasoning and mix lightly to a dough. Roll out about ¼″ thick and cut into shapes. Brush with beaten egg and bake in a moderately hot oven (Reg. 6, 400 °F.) for about 10 minutes till golden brown. Cool slightly before moving from tray.

Devilled Biscuits*

Use water biscuits or oatcakes as a base for devilled biscuits.

2 oz butter or margarine
2 teaspoons chutney
Worcester sauce
plain biscuits

Mix the ingredients together to form a paste and spread it thinly on plain biscuits. Pop into a brisk oven (Reg. 6, 400 °F.) for 5 minutes and eat them hot.

Oatcakes

1 lb medium ground oatmeal
3 oz flour
pinch bicarbonate of soda
salt
3 oz dripping or lard
pinch sugar
boiling water

Warm the utensils and mix the dry ingredients together. Rub in the fat and make the whole into a stiff dough with the boiling water. Roll out quickly on a floured board, stamp into rounds and bake in a hot oven (Reg. 6, 400 °F.) for 15 to 20 minutes.

Peanut Cookies*

Nearly all children love salted peanuts, so try incorporating them in your cooking as they do in America.

8 oz rolled oats
4 oz sugar
4 oz flour
4 oz salted peanuts – crushed
4 oz margarine
1 tablespoon treacle
1 egg or a little milk

Mix all the dry ingredients together, make a well in the centre and add the egg (or milk), treacle and melted margarine. Mix well together and form into small cakes about ¼" thick. Place on greased tins and bake in a moderate oven (Reg. 4, 355 °F.) for about 25 minutes.

Walnut Sablés*

3 oz margarine
3 oz plain flour
3 oz grated cheese
seasoning
2 oz chopped walnuts
1 egg

Rub the margarine into the sifted flour and add the cheese and seasoning. Work into a paste and roll out ¼" thick. Cut into strips 2" wide. Brush with beaten egg, sprinkle thickly with walnuts and a little salt and cut each strip into triangles. Place on a greased baking sheet and bake in a moderate oven (Reg. 4, 355 °F.) for 7 to 10 minutes until a rich, golden brown.

Water Biscuits*

½ lb flour
½ teaspoon salt
1 teaspoon baking powder
2 oz fat
water
ground rock or sea salt

Sift the flour with the salt and baking powder and rub in

the fat. Form into a firm dough with some water. Roll out very thinly, prick and stamp into large rounds. Sprinkle with the salt and bake in a slow oven (Reg. 2, 310 °F.) for about 20 minutes until pale gold.

Sweet Biscuits

Again these are easy to make and economical.

Almond Wafers*

In France these are called *tuiles* (tiles) because they are traditionally baked and served in the curved, overlapping manner of Southern French and Spanish roof tiles.

3 oz ground almonds
2 oz sugar
2 oz butter or margarine
1 tablespoon flour
2 tablespoons milk

Cream all the ingredients together and drop in teaspoonsful well apart on a greased and floured baking sheet. Bake in a moderate oven (Reg. 4, 355 °F.) for about 10 minutes until lightly browned. Cool slightly then lay over rolling pin to shape so that they are curved when cold.

Anzac Biscuits*

A good, solid, chewy biscuit.

3 oz rolled oats
3 oz flour
4 oz sugar
3 oz desiccated coconut
1 tablespoon syrup
2 oz margarine
1½ teaspoons bicarbonate of soda
2 tablespoons boiling water

Mix the oats, flour, sugar and coconut together. Melt the syrup and margarine in a pan over gentle heat. Dissolve the bicarbonate of soda in the boiling water and add to the margarine and syrup then combine with the dry ingredients. Drop in tablespoonsful on to a greased baking sheet and cook in a slow oven (Reg. 2, 310°F.) for about 20 minutes.

Arrowroot Biscuits*

A plain and simple biscuit to serve with mousses and ices.

4 oz butter or margarine
2 eggs
4 oz caster sugar
4 oz flour
3 oz ground arrowroot

Cream the butter or margarine. Whisk the eggs and beat them into the creamed butter a little at a time. Stir in the sugar gradually and beat well. Sift the arrowroot with the flour and mix in. Drop in very small mounds on to a greased tin and bake in a slow oven (Reg. 2, 310°F.) for about 15 minutes.

Biscuit Crunch*

Useful if you have a lot of broken or slightly stale biscuits which should be used up.

2 oz syrup
2 oz margarine
2 oz chocolate
2 oz sugar
1 dessertspoon cocoa
4 oz sweet biscuits

Melt the margarine and syrup with the chocolate over gentle heat. Add the sugar and cocoa and cool slightly before stirring in the broken-up biscuits. Press into a greased sandwich tin and leave in a warm oven, after the heat has been turned off, until the mixture is cold and set. Cut into wedges after a few hours and sprinkle with caster sugar.

Bosworth Jumbles*

8 oz wholemeal flour
6 oz margarine
8 oz caster sugar
1 egg

Rub the margarine into the flour with the fingertips. Beat the egg and the sugar together and add to the flour to make an elastic dough. Bosworth Jumbles are traditionally baked in an 'S' shape so roll the dough into 4" long strips between the palms of the hands and arrange each one in an 'S' on a greased baking sheet. Cook in a moderate oven (Reg. 4, 355 °F.) for about 15 minutes.

Butter Leaves*

A delicate cookie from Sweden.

4 oz butter
2 oz sugar
1 egg
7 oz flour
1 oz chopped nuts (walnuts, hazelnuts or almonds)
2 extra tablespoons sugar

Cream the butter and sugar together until fluffy. Mix in the yolk of the egg and the flour. Chill. Roll out thinly and cut into shapes. Brush with the beaten egg white and sprinkle with the nuts and the extra sugar. Place on a buttered baking sheet and bake in a moderate oven (Reg. 4, 355 °F.) for about 10 minutes.

Butterscotch Biscuits*

10 oz flour
salt
2 teaspoons baking powder
2 oz lard

1 oz butter or margarine
approximately 8 tablespoons milk
For the butterscotch:
4 oz butter
4 oz brown sugar

Rub the fats into the dry ingredients and stir in the milk to make a soft dough. Knead and roll out ½″ thick. Spread with half the butterscotch mixture of brown sugar and butter worked together. Roll up and cut into ½″-thick slices. Spread the rest of the butterscotch mixture on to a greased baking sheet and place the rolls of dough flat upon it. Bake in a hot oven (Reg. 6, 400 °F.) for 12 to 15 minutes and remove from the tin at once before the butterscotch has time to harden.

Chocolate Crinkles*

3½ tablespoons corn oil
2 oz cooking chocolate, melted
1 level teaspoon cocoa
6½ oz caster sugar
2 eggs
vanilla essence
5 oz flour
1 level teaspoon baking powder
½ level teaspoon salt
icing sugar

Mix the oil with the chocolate, cocoa and sugar. Beat in the eggs one at a time and add a few drops of vanilla essence. Sift together the flour, baking powder and salt and fold into the chocolate mixture. Cover and chill overnight then roll into little balls and toss in sifted icing sugar. Place 2″ apart on a baking sheet lined with greaseproof paper. Bake in a moderate oven (Reg. 4, 355 °F.) for about 10 minutes and allow to cool slightly before removing from tray.

Chocolate Crisps*

The addition of coffee enhances the flavour of these chocolate crisps.

4 oz chocolate
3 tablespoons Puffed Wheat or Rice Crispies
1 teaspoon cocoa
1 tablespoon instant coffee

Melt the chocolate in a saucepan over gentle heat. Beat it smooth and stir in the Puffed Wheat or Rice Crispies together with the cocoa and coffee. Put out on greaseproof paper in little rough heaps and leave till firm.

Coconut Macaroons

Useful when you have egg whites left over – perhaps after having used the yolks in soup or sauces. Rice paper can be bought in good bakers' shops.

4 oz caster sugar
2 whites of egg
3 oz dessicated coconut
vanilla essence
rice paper

Cover a baking sheet with rice paper. Put the egg whites and sugar into a bowl and whisk over a pan of hot water until very thick and white. Remove from the heat and stir in the coconut and a few drops of vanilla essence. Place in spoonfuls on the rice paper and bake in a cool oven (Reg. 1, 290 °F.) for $\frac{3}{4}$ to 1 hour. They should not brown. Remove from the tin and trim the rice paper away cleanly from the edge of each macaroon.

Coconut Rings*

4 oz flour
4 oz caster sugar
4 oz butter or margarine
4 oz desiccated coconut
1 beaten egg
raspberry jam

Mix the flour with the sugar and rub in the butter or

94

margarine. Stir in the coconut and egg. Knead lightly then roll out thinly. Cut into rounds with a 2½″ plain cutter then remove the centres with a smaller cutter. Bake in a moderate oven (Reg. 4, 355 °F.) for about 15 minutes and sandwich together with raspberry jam when cool.

Coffee Sandwich Biscuits*

3 oz margarine
2 oz caster sugar
2 level teaspoons instant coffee
1 teaspoon water
3 oz flour
1 oz ground rice
halved walnuts

Cream the margarine and sugar together until light and fluffy then add the coffee powder blended with the water. Fold in the sifted flour and ground rice and knead lightly on a floured board. Roll out thinly and cut into 2″ rounds. Place a walnut half on every other biscuit. Lay on a greased baking sheet and bake in a moderate oven (Reg. 4, 355 °F.) for 15 minutes – till just coloured. Cool and sandwich together with coffee butter cream.

Crack-a-Jack*

An old favourite which is particularly easy to make and a great standby.

4 oz margarine
1 oz sugar
2 tablespoons syrup
8 oz rolled oats
salt

Melt the margarine with the sugar and syrup in a saucepan over gentle heat. Remove and stir in the oats and salt. Mix well and press into Swiss-roll tin lined with greased paper. Bake in a moderate oven (Reg. 4, 355 °F.) for about 30 minutes till golden brown. Cut into fingers and leave in the tin until cold.

Digestive Biscuits*

6 oz wholemeal flour
1 oz oatmeal
½ teaspoon salt
1 oz flour
2 oz sugar
1 teaspoon baking powder
3 oz butter or margarine
milk to bind

Rub the fat into the dry ingredients and add just enough milk to bind. Knead well and roll out thinly. Stamp into rounds, prick with a fork and bake in a moderate oven (Reg. 4, 355 °F.) for about 15 minutes

Easter Biscuits*

One of the few traditional Easter recipes in this country.

4 oz butter or margarine
4 oz caster sugar
8 oz flour
2 oz currants
1 egg
¼ teaspoon nutmeg
½ teaspoon cinnamon

Cream the butter or margarine with the sugar and then work in the other ingredients. Roll out thinly and cut into rounds with a fluted cutter. Bake in a moderate oven (Reg. 4, 355 °F.) for 10 to 15 minutes.

Fruity Ginger Biscuits*

4 oz margarine
4 oz brown sugar
8 oz flour
2 level teaspoons ground ginger

1 level teaspoon ground cinnamon
1 level teaspoon bicarbonate of soda
2 oz syrup
3 oz currants
approximately 3 tablespoons milk
split almonds

Cream the margarine and the sugar. Sift together the flour, spices and bicarbonate of soda and stir into the creamed mixture with the warm syrup, the currants and enough milk to give a fairly soft dough. Place in teaspoonsful on a greased baking sheet allowing room to spread. Put a split almond on each and bake in a moderate oven (Reg. 4, 355 °F.) for about 20 minutes. Cool slightly before removing from tray.

Haman's Ears

A long time ago an over-enthusiastic grocer delivered one pound of poppy seeds instead of the modest one ounce that I had ordered. Then the children went down with mumps and I never got round to returning the surplus so I was delighted to come across this funny little recipe which, over the years, has succeeded in considerably reducing my stock of poppy seeds. They are strange but toothsome confections.

3 oz curd cheese
2 oz butter or margarine, softened
4 oz flour
about 6 tablespoons milk
1½ oz poppy seeds
1 tablespoon honey
1 tablespoon sugar
1 egg
salt

Beat together the curd cheese, the butter or margarine and a pinch of salt. Sift in the flour and knead into a ball. Chill for 2 to 3 hours then pinch off little nuts of the dough and form into small 'ears' with the edges raised to hold the filling.

Make the filling by mixing together in a small saucepan the poppy seeds, milk, honey, sugar and a pinch of salt. Cook gently until it thickens then beat in the egg. Fill the ears with the mixture and bake in a moderate oven (Reg. 4, 355 °F.) for 12 to 15 minutes.

Janhagel*
Spicy Dutch biscuits.

4 oz butter or margarine
6 oz flour
2 oz caster sugar
½ level teaspoon cinnamon
1 oz flaked almonds
a little granulated sugar

Rub the butter or margarine into the sieved flour. Add the caster sugar and cinnamon and work together. Roll out to form a rectangle then press into a buttered baking tin (approximately 6″ by 10″). Smooth with a knife and sprinkle with the almonds and granulated sugar. Bake in a moderate oven (Reg. 4, 355 °F.) for about 20 minutes and cut into fingers while still warm. Cool on a wire rack.

Lemon Wafers*
6 oz butter or margarine
6 oz sugar
8 oz flour
¼ teaspoon bicarbonate of soda
¼ teaspoon salt
2 eggs
1 lemon

Cream the butter or margarine with the sugar, add the eggs then add the flour sifted with the salt and the bicarbonate of soda, the grated rind of the lemon and 1 tablespoon of its juice. Roll out thinly, cut into rounds and bake in a moderate oven (Reg. 4, 355 °F.) for about 10 minutes.

Melting Moments*

Very simple but surprisingly good.

2½ oz lard
1½ oz margarine
3 oz caster sugar
½ egg
1 teaspoon vanilla essence
5 oz self raising flour
rolled oats
glacé cherries

Cream the fats with the sugar and beat in the half egg. Work in the flour and vanilla essence. Roll into small balls with wet hands and coat with rolled oats. Place well apart on greased baking trays, press out slightly and put half a glacé cherry on each. Bake in a moderate oven (Reg. 4, 355 °F.) for 15 to 20 minutes and cool before moving.

Orange Drops*

5 oz margarine or whipped-up cooking fat
5 oz caster sugar
1 egg
6 tablespoons orange juice
2 level tablespoons grated orange rind
8 oz flour
½ level teaspoon baking powder
½ level teaspoon bicarbonate of soda

Beat together the fat, sugar and egg until smooth. Stir in the orange juice and rind alternately with the flour sifted with the baking powder and bicarbonate of soda. When well blended, drop in teaspoonsful on to a greased baking sheet leaving plenty of space between them. Flatten to about ¼″ thickness and dredge with caster sugar. Bake in a hot oven (Reg. 6, 400 °F.) for about 10 minutes. Cool a little before moving from tin and, if preferred, sandwich together with orange butter cream.

Orange Jumbles*

4 oz almonds
4 oz sugar
3 oz butter or margarine
2 oz flour
2 oranges

Shred the almonds and mix them with the sugar and butter or margarine, flour and the grated rind and juice of the oranges. Drop the mixture in teaspoonsful on to a greased baking sheet, leaving space for them to spread. Bake in a fairly slow oven (Reg. 3, 330 °F.) for about 20 minutes.

Peanut Butter Cookies*

Crunchy and always popular.

2 oz crunchy peanut butter
2 oz butter or margarine
grated rind ½ orange
1½ oz brown sugar
2 oz caster sugar
½ egg
1½ oz sultanas
4 oz self raising flour

Cream together the peanut butter and butter or margarine, orange rind and sugars. Beat in the egg, add the sultanas and stir in the sifted flour. Roll into balls the size of walnuts and place well apart on an ungreased baking sheet. Bake in a moderate oven (Reg. 4, 355 °F.) for about 25 minutes.

Ragged Robins*

2 egg whites
¼ teaspoon salt
8 oz sugar
1 teaspoon vanilla essence
3 oz chopped walnuts
3 oz chopped dates
3 oz crushed cornflakes

Beat the egg whites until light and gradually add the sugar, salt and vanilla then fold in the nuts, dates and cornflakes. Drop from a teaspoon on to a buttered baking sheet and cook for about 30 minutes in a cool oven (Reg. 2, 310 °F.).

Rice Biscuits*

Nice biscuits because of their fine, grainy texture. Very good with ices.

¼ lb caster sugar
¼ lb butter or margarine
½ lb ground rice
1 egg

Cream the butter or margarine and stir in the sugar, ground rice and beaten egg. Roll out and cut into very small rounds. Bake in a slow oven (Reg. 2, 310°F.) for about 15 minutes.

Shortbread*

However heavy-handed your young cooks may be, they won't harm this excellent shortbread. It can be flavoured with cocoa, coffee powder or grated orange rind for variety.

5 oz flour
1 oz ground rice
2 oz caster sugar
4 oz butter or margarine

Sieve the flour and ground rice into a bowl, add the sugar and fat and knead together. Press into a tin lined with grease-proof paper. Prick with a fork, crimp up the edges and bake in a cool oven (Reg. 3, 330 °F.) for ¾ to 1 hour. Remove and cut into wedges or fingers and dredge with caster sugar when cold.

Sugar Thins

A very elegant biscuit.

8 oz butter
8 oz caster sugar
1 egg
1 tablespoon cream

10 oz flour
½ teaspoon salt
1 teaspoon baking powder
vanilla essence (or lemon juice or ground ginger)

Cream the butter and sugar together then work in the other ingredients. Firm in the fridge overnight. Roll out as thinly as possible on a lightly floured board. Cut into rounds, sprinkle with caster sugar and bake in a moderately hot oven (Reg. 5, 375 °F.) for 5 minutes. These biscuits should remain pale.

6. CAKES

Here are some recipes for plainer cakes (which the children can make) and for a selection of individual cakes as well as for the large prettily decorated cakes that are still a major attraction at a children's party.

Plain Cakes

Applesauce Cake*
If you are lucky enough to have apple trees in the garden

this is a good way of using up windfalls. It makes a rich, dark, sticky cake.

8 oz flour
2 teaspoons bicarbonate of soda
¼ teaspoon salt
2 teaspoons cinnamon
1½ teaspoons powdered cloves
4 oz chopped nuts
4 oz mixed dried fruit
2 oz margarine
4 oz brown sugar
2 eggs
2 cups apple purée

Sift together the flour, bicarbonate of soda, salt and spices and mix about 1 cupful with the nuts and dried fruits. Cream the margarine and gradually beat in the sugar and then the eggs. Add the flour mixture alternately with the apple purée then beat in the fruit-nut mixture. Bake in a lined 8″ tin in a moderate oven (Reg. 4, 355 °F.) for about 1 hour.

Fruit Loaf*
Quick and easy to make and very economical. Slice and butter it.

6 oz self raising flour
½ teaspoon mixed spice
¼ teaspoon nutmeg
1 oz lard
4 oz mixed dried fruit
3 oz caster sugar
1 tablespoon treacle
about ¼ pint milk

Sift the flour with the mixed spice and nutmeg then rub in the lard. Stir in the sugar, dried fruit and treacle and add the milk to make a dropping consistency. Bake in a lined loaf tin 8″ by 4″ in a moderate oven (Reg. 4, 355 °F.) for about 40 minutes.

Gingerbread*

A time-honoured favourite to be eaten plain or spread with butter.

4 oz margarine
9 oz treacle or syrup
4 oz sugar (brown or white)
10 oz flour
1 level teaspoon bicarbonate of soda
½ level teaspoon salt
1 teaspoon ground ginger
1 teaspoon cinnamon
1 egg
about ¼ pint milk

Melt the fat with the treacle or syrup and sugar over gentle heat. Sift the flour, bicarbonate of soda, salt and spices into a bowl, hollow out the centre and add the beaten egg and milk, then pour in the syrup mixture. Beat until smooth, pour into a lined loaf tin 9" by 5" and bake in a slow oven (Reg. 3, 330 °F.) for about 1½ hours.

Orange Tea Bread*

4 oz margarine
10 oz self raising flour
½ level teaspoon salt
3 tablespoons clear honey
grated rind of 1 orange
1 egg
2 tablespoons marmalade
4 tablespoons milk

Place all the ingredients together in a bowl and beat until well mixed. Place in a lined 2 lb loaf tin and bake in a moderate oven (Reg. 4, 355 °F.) for 1¼ to 1½ hours.

Parkin*

Similar to gingerbread but denser and less sweet. It is excellent with cheese for winter picnics and should be made a day or two before it is needed.

12 oz medium oatmeal
6 oz flour
1 tablespoon sugar
½ teaspoon ground ginger
¼ teaspoon salt
4 oz margarine
1 lb treacle
4 tablespoons milk
½ teaspoon bicarbonate of soda

Mix the oatmeal, flour, sugar, ginger and salt well. Warm the treacle and margarine together then warm the milk separately with the bicarbonate of soda. Mix altogether, pour into a bottom-lined roasting tin and bake in a moderate oven (Reg. 4, 355 °F.) for about 45 minutes. Cut into squares while still warm.

Tea Brack*

A North Country speciality which is simple to make.

½ pint cold tea
1 lb mixed dried fruit
8 oz brown sugar
1 lb self raising flour
4 tablespoons milk

Soak the fruit and sugar overnight in the tea. Next day sift in the flour, add the milk, beat well and pour into a lined 2 lb loaf tin. Bake in a moderate oven (Reg. 4, 355 °F.) for about 2 hours and serve thinly sliced and spread with butter.

Small Cakes

Apple Slices

A sort of super apple pie cut into manageable teatime fingers.

8 oz short crust pastry
2 large cooking apples
2 tablespoons sugar

pinch mixed spice
1 oz grated cheese

Line a 7″-square tin with half the pastry and spread the sliced apples on it. Sprinkle with the sugar, spice and cheese. Cover with the rest of the pastry, press the edges together and seal. Brush with cold water and sprinkle with caster sugar. Bake in a hot oven (Reg. 6, 400 °F.) for 10 minutes then reduce to moderate (Reg. 4, 355 °F.) for a further 20 minutes. Leave to cool and cut into slices.

Fruit Scones*

8 oz flour
2 teaspoons baking powder
½ teaspoon salt
1 oz margarine
1 oz sugar
¼ pint of milk or 1 egg and a little less milk
2 oz dried fruit

Sieve the flour with the salt, sugar and baking powder then rub in the fat. Stir in the fruit and mix to a soft dough with the milk or egg and milk. Knead lightly. Roll out to ¾″ thickness and stamp into small rounds. Brush over with milk or beaten egg. Place on a baking sheet and bake in a hot oven (Reg. 7, 425 °F.) for 5 minutes then reduce to moderate heat (Reg. 5, 375 °F.) and continue baking for another 5 minutes. Cool on a wire rack.

Ginger Buns*

3 oz margarine
3 oz brown sugar
3 tablespoons treacle
¼ pint milk
8 oz flour
2 teaspoons ground ginger
½ teaspoon mixed spice
1 teaspoon bicarbonate of soda
3 oz sultanas

Gently heat the treacle, margarine, sugar and milk together and allow to cool then stir in the dry ingredients sifted together and the sultanas. Mix well, put into greased patty tins and bake in a moderate oven (Reg. 4, 355 °F.) for 15 to 20 minutes.

Mint Cakes

Rather like Eccles Cakes but with an interesting difference.

8 oz short crust pastry
6 oz currants
1 oz butter
2 oz caster sugar
1 tablespoon finely chopped fresh mint

Roll out the pastry and cut it into 3″ rounds. Mix all the ingredients together and place in spoonfuls on the centre of the pastry rounds. Draw the edges together, turn each cake over and flatten it slightly. Brush with beaten egg, sprinkle with a little sugar and bake in a hot oven (Reg. 6, 400 °F.) for about 15 minutes.

Orange Cakes*

After chocolate, orange seems to be the second favourite flavour with most children.

3 oz butter or margarine
3 oz caster sugar
2 eggs or 1 egg and 3 tablespoons milk
4½ oz flour
½ teaspoon baking powder
1 orange

Cream the butter or margarine and sugar together and add the beaten eggs or beaten egg and milk gradually, beating well. Lightly stir in the sifted flour and baking powder together with the grated rind of the orange. Lastly stir in the juice of half the orange and divide the mixture between 12 small patty tins. Bake in a fairly hot oven (Reg. 6, 400 °F.) for 10 minutes then turn the tin around, reduce the heat slightly and bake for a further 10 minutes. When cold, top with a little orange-flavoured icing and decorate with hundreds and thousands or a slice of crystallized orange.

Orange Tartlets

These tartlets have an excellent filling – light and fresh tasting.

8 oz short crust pastry
3 oz butter or margarine
3 oz sugar
2 eggs
2 oranges
½ teaspoon vanilla essence

Line small patty tins with the pastry. Cream the butter and sugar well together, beat in each egg yolk separately and add the grated rind of the oranges, 2 tablespoons of the juice and the vanilla essence. Whisk the white of 1 egg stiffly and stir it lightly into the mixture. Pile into the pastry cases and bake in a moderate oven (Reg. 4, 355 °F.) for 15 to 20 minutes dredging the tartlets with caster sugar after 10 minutes cooking.

Rum Truffles*

Mouth-watering confections to make when you have some stale cake or broken biscuits to use up.

3 oz chocolate
1 oz butter
1 egg
6 oz cake or biscuit crumbs
rum essence
chocolate vermicelli

Melt the chocolate and butter together over gentle heat. Cool slightly then stir in the beaten egg, crumbs and rum essence to taste. Beat well, form into small balls and roll in chocolate vermicelli (or finely grated chocolate or mixed cocoa and icing sugar). Leave to firm.

Scotch Pancakes*

These are fun for children to make and are best eaten on the same day spread with butter and jam or honey.

8 oz flour
½ teaspoon bicarbonate of soda
1 teaspoon cream of tartar
pinch of salt
1 tablespoon syrup
2 eggs
about ¼ pint of milk

Sift the dry ingredients into a bowl, make a well in the centre and add the syrup, beaten eggs and milk. Mix to a thick batter stirring lightly. Drop from a teaspoon into a hot, greased frying pan. After a few minutes turn them over with a palette knife and cook the other side.

Welsh Cakes*

8 oz flour
pinch of salt
1 teaspoon baking powder
2 oz caster sugar
2 oz margarine
2 oz lard
4 oz mixed dried fruit
1 egg
a little milk

Sift the dry ingredients together and rub in the fat. Stir in the dried fruit and mix to a stiff dough with the egg and milk. Roll out to about ¼″ thickness, stamp into rounds and cook slowly in a hot, greased frying pan until golden brown on each side.

Centrepiece Cakes

Chocolate Cake

This is an extremely good cake – finely textured and slightly grainy. It should be made the day before it is needed.

6 oz chocolate
2 tablespoons milk
6 oz butter or margarine
4½ oz caster sugar
3 eggs
4 oz flour
2 oz ground rice
¾ teaspoon baking powder
½ teaspoon vanilla essence

Melt the chocolate in the milk over low heat and leave to cool. Cream the butter or margarine and sugar together and stir in the chocolate when it is cold. Beat in the eggs a little at a time then lightly stir in the sifted flour, ground rice and baking powder and add the vanilla essence. Pour into a lined 8″ cake tin and bake in a moderate oven (Reg. 4, 355 °F.) for about 1 hour. The following day split the cake and sandwich it with whipped cream or butter icing and coat the top with chocolate glacé icing. Decorate with whorls of cream, nuts, crystallized violets, crystallized rose petals, chocolate vermicelli or grated chocolate.

Coffee and Honey Cake

A delicious combination of tastes and a light spongy texture.

6 oz self raising flour
2 level teaspoons baking powder
pinch of salt
2 oz caster sugar
6 oz margarine, Trex or Cookeen
3 eggs
2 level teaspoons instant coffee
4 level tablespoons honey

Sieve flour, baking powder and salt into a basin and add the sugar, fat, eggs, coffee and honey. Beat until smooth and pour into two lined 8″ sandwich tins. Bake in a moderate oven (Reg. 4, 355 °F.) for about 30 minutes. Cool and sandwich together with coffee butter cream and mask with coffee glacé icing. Decorate with walnut halves.

Devil's Food Cake

A loosely woven, sticky chocolate cake.

6 oz flour
¼ level teaspoon baking powder
1 level teaspoon bicarbonate of soda
¼ level teaspoon salt
2 oz cocoa
8 fluid oz cold water (12 tablespoons)
4 oz butter or margarine
10 oz caster sugar
2 eggs, beaten

Sift the flour with the baking powder, bicarbonate of soda and salt. Blend the cocoa with the water. Cream the fat, add the sugar and beat thoroughly. Add the eggs a little at a time and beat well. Stir in the sifted flour alternately with the cocoa mixture. Divide between 2 lined 8″ sandwich tins and bake in a moderate oven (Reg. 4, 355 °F.) for about 30 minutes. Sandwich together with chocolate butter icing and coat with chocolate glacé icing. Decorate with chocolate leaves (*see* p. 128).

Dundee Cake

Young children never seem particularly interested in fruit cake, but the older ones like it – particularly boys.

6 oz butter or margarine
6 oz caster sugar
4 eggs
6 oz flour
1 lb mixed dried fruit

4 oz glacé cherries
½ lemon
1 level teaspoon baking powder
1 oz almonds
a little milk sweetened with sugar

Cream the butter or margarine and sugar thoroughly then beat in the eggs one at a time adding a little of the flour with each. Add the dried fruit, the halved cherries and the grated rind and juice of the lemon, then stir in the rest of the flour sifted with the baking powder. Turn into a lined cake tin (7″ in diameter) and bake in a moderately slow oven (Reg. 3, 330 °F.) for 1½ to 2 hours. After 1 hour scatter the split almonds over the top and, about 10 minutes before it is ready, brush with heavily sweetened milk.

Fruit Flan

French open fruit flans can form glamorous centrepieces for a lunch or tea table and make the most of the finest fruit in season. To show them off to best effect you need a shallow flan tin about 9″ in diameter – preferably fluted and with a detachable base.

6 oz flour
3 oz butter or margarine
3 oz caster sugar
1 egg yolk
water
few drops of vanilla essence
little grated lemon rind
fruit in season

Rub the butter or margarine into the flour and add the other ingredients making a fairly stiff dough. Line the flan tin with the pastry and bake it blind in a hot oven. When cold, arrange the fruit in circles inside it – raspberries, halved strawberries or cherries, sliced peaches, apricots, greengages, sweet plums or grapes are all ideal because they do not need cooking. Sprinkle a little caster sugar over them and then *glaze* them. This is important or they will not look attractive. To glaze: boil 3 tablespoons of the associated jam (or red-currant or apricot jam which go quite well with everything) with 3 tablespoons of water for a few minutes. Sieve, then mix in 3 teaspoons of powdered arrowroot mixed to a cream with 3 more tablespoons of water. Boil again for a few minutes stirring all the time then pour, while still hot, over the fruit. This will set to a clear, firm jelly.

Galette des Rois

Traditional French recipes for Twelfth Night cake are so extraordinarily complicated – and produce such an un-believably dull cake – that I usually compromise with my version of a Victorian Sand cake. This produces a close-knit, lemony cake which you can coat with a lemon icing and decorate with little figures of the three kings or with crowns or stars cut out of crystallized lemon. The whole point of a Galette des Rois is the treasure hidden inside it, for the one who finds the treasure is king for the day. Treasure can be a coin (well washed) or a little plastic or metal charm or trinket. In France you can buy tiny things specially made for the Galette des Rois.

8 oz butter
grated rind of 1 lemon
5 oz sifted icing sugar
3 oz self raising flour
3 oz ground rice or cornflour
6 egg yolks
3 egg whites
extra sifted icing sugar

Cream the butter and grated lemon rind and then beat in the icing sugar. Sift the flour and ground rice or cornflour together and add one third of it to the creamed mixture. Add 2 of the egg yolks and repeat twice more with the remaining flour and yolks. Fold in the stiffly whisked whites and turn into buttered and floured tin. Bake in a moderate oven (Reg. 4, 355 °F.) for 1 hour.

Gingerbread House

This always makes a tremendous impression but is really quite easy to make and very inexpensive. For the gingerbread mixture you will need:

1 lb margarine
6 oz sifted icing sugar
1 lb self raising flour
1 teaspoon salt
2 teaspoons ground ginger
vanilla essence
6 oz rolled oats

Beat the margarine and blend in the sifted icing sugar. Work in the flour sieved with the ginger and salt and mix in a few drops of vanilla essence. Add the oats to form a stiff dough which can be rolled out to a thickness of $\frac{1}{4}''$.

To make the house: find a smallish shoe box to use as the frame and you will have no trouble in making the house stand up. Lay the long side of the box upon your rolled out dough and cut around it with a sharp knife to make the front wall of the house then cut out a second piece the same size for the back wall. Now up-end the box on the dough and cut around three sides of the shorter end. Remove the box and finish off this end wall by extending the two sides up to a pointed gable. Cut another end wall to match. Cut two square pieces for the roof with each side measuring the same as the longer side of the box. You now have six pieces of dough. Lay them on a baking sheet and, with a small, sharp knife, cut out a door and two windows in the front wall (place the door on the baking sheet to be cooked as well), and windows only on the back and end walls. Now bake the gingerbread in a slow oven (Reg. 3, 330 °F.) for about 20 minutes. Prepare a small bowl of glacé icing (just icing sugar and water mixed to a thick cream) to use as glue. Put a couple of dabs on the bottom of the box and affix it to whatever you want to use as a base – pastry board or small tray. In the box put tiny presents for each of the children and on top pile crumpled tissue paper which will help to support the roof.

When the gingerbread is cooked and cool pipe icing around the windows and door to look like snow. Stick red Cellophane on the inside of the windows by dabbing a little icing round the edge. Now you can start constructing the house by standing the four walls of it leaning ever so slightly against the sides of the box and pipe icing down the corners to fill in the gaps and hold the walls together. Pipe a thick line along the top edge of the walls and embed the roof in this – rather like making a card house – and fix the front door in place slightly ajar with a ridge of icing down one side. When set it will all be quite firm.

Frost on the roof can be simulated by brushing with egg white and scattering caster sugar on top. Sugar or cotton wool spread around the base will enhance the effect and any little fir trees, robins, tiny deer which you happen to have will all help. When the time comes to dismember it, start by removing the roof with a sharp knife, so revealing the treasure.

Maypole Cake

I boast 100 per cent failure with Victoria sponges but this Genoese sponge never lets me down and is the ideal base for a Maypole Cake and for many other sorts of sandwich cake.

1½ oz clarified butter
2½ oz flour
½ oz cornflour
3 large eggs
4 oz caster sugar

Clarify the butter by melting it slowly and then continuing to heat gently until all the bubbling has ceased. Let it cool for a few minutes while the sediment sinks to the bottom, then pour off the fat. Sift the flour and cornflour together. Put the eggs and sugar into a basin, stand it over a pan of hot water and whisk until light and thick. Remove from the heat. Sift half the flour over the surface and fold in very lightly. Add the remaining flour in the same way alternately with the cooled, clarified butter. Pour into two lined 8″ sandwich tins and bake in a moderate oven (Reg. 4, 355 °F.) for about 30 minutes, until golden brown and firm to the touch.

For a Maypole Cake, sandwich the two sponges together with butter cream and mask in glacé icing coloured very pale green. Find some thick wool in five different colours and cut a 20″ length of each. Holding the ends even tie a loose loop in the centre and slip this around a 10″ knitting needle, pull tight and push the knitting needle right through the centre of the cake until it touches the plate. Separate the strands of wool evenly around the edge of the cake and keep in place by pressing a jelly baby firmly into the icing on the end of each strand.

Mocha Cake

Easy to make and luscious to eat.

8 trifle sponge cakes
1 oz granulated sugar
2 teaspoons instant coffee
3 oz unsalted butter
1 egg yolk
3 oz icing sugar
1 oz almonds, walnuts or chocolate vermicelli

Make one cup of coffee with the sugar and the coffee powder. Let it go cold. Cream the butter and sifted icing sugar together and beat in the egg yolk. Mix in about half the cold coffee very gradually. Soak each sponge cake in coffee, squeeze it out and pack closely side by side in a row. Spread about one third of the cream on them then add another layer of soaked sponge. Mask with the cream, decorate and let the cake stand for 24 hours .To be eaten with pastry fork or teaspoon.

Pineapple Flan

large tin pineapple pieces or crushed pineapple
½ oz caster sugar
2 eggs
8 oz short crust pastry

Line a sandwich tin with the pastry and bake it blind. Strain the pineapple and put $\frac{1}{4}$ pint of the syrup into a small saucepan with the sugar. Bring to the boil and simmer for 5 minutes. Cool slightly then add the beaten egg yolks and cook gently until the mixture thickens, stirring frequently. Place the pineapple in the pastry case, cover with the custard and spread the stiffly whisked egg whites on top. Decorate with halved glacé cherries and little spikes of angelica, and bake in a cool oven until the meringue is crisp and pale gold. Serve cold as a cake.

7. DRINKS, ICES AND SWEETMEATS

Drinks

Blackcurrant Cordial

Make this when you have a bumper crop of blackcurrants in the garden or access to an inexpensive supply. The fruit must be very ripe.

2 lb blackcurrants
1 pint water
sugar

Wash the fruit. Put it into a saucepan with the water, bring to the boil and boil fast for 1 minute. Strain through muslin and press to extract all the juice. Stir in ¾ lb sugar for every pint of juice. Pour into bottles filling them to about

$1\frac{1}{2}''$ from the top. Put on corks or screw tops and stand the bottles *on* something (a wooden board or a tin plate or lid) in a large saucepan or preserving pan. Fill the pan with warm water up to the level of the juice in the bottles, bring to the boil and simmer for 20 minutes. Dilute to use. Unopened this keeps almost indefinitely in a cool place, but once opened store in the refrigerator and use up in a week or two.

Cider*

This is fun to make and produces a quite refreshing, fizzy drink. It needs to be made at least one week before it is required and tastes even better if it can be left for a month or two.

3 lb cooking apples
12 pints cold water
2 lb sugar
3 lemons

Wash the apples, cut up roughly and mince complete with cores and skins. Place in an earthenware bowl or white plastic bucket and pour on the water. Cover and leave for 1 week, stirring night and morning. Strain, stir in the sugar and the grated rind and juice of the lemons. Set aside for 24 hours then strain and bottle in screw-topped flagons. If keeping it for some weeks you should cautiously loosen the tops now and then to relieve the pressure which builds up inside the bottles.

Coffee-Chocolate

A warming and unusual drink after a cold winter outing.

1½ pints milk
1 pint coffee
4 oz plain chocolate
3 tablespoons sugar
vanilla essence
whipping cream (optional)

In a large jug mix the coffee and 1 pint of the milk (heated) together and keep hot. Melt the chocolate in 2 tablespoons of water over gentle heat. Heat the remaining ½ pint of milk with the sugar. Add a few drops of vanilla essence and stir into the melted chocolate, then combine this mixture with the hot coffee and serve, topped, if you feel lavish, with a dollop of whipped cream.

Coffee – Iced

So many children nowadays like coffee that they will love this on a hot summer day. You *can* use instant coffee, but real ground coffee has far more flavour. Sweeten the black coffee while it is still hot so that the sugar will dissolve and then chill it thoroughly. When cold, stir in plenty of chilled milk. Keep in a jug in the fridge until required and at the last minute you can, if you like, top it with thin cream whisked to a froth.

Fruit Squash

This is a basic recipe. It is simplicity itself to make and keeps quite well in a fridge or cool larder for 2 or 3 weeks.

2 oranges
2 lemons
2 lb sugar
1 oz tartaric acid (from chemist)
2 pints water

Cut up the fruit, mix with the sugar, pour on the boiling water and stir well together. Leave to stand overnight then strain and mix in the tartaric acid. Bottle and dilute before use.

Lemon Barley Water

2 oz pearl barley
approximately 1 oz sugar
1 lemon
1 pint boiling water

Blanch the barley by covering it with cold water in a pan,

bringing it to the boil and boiling for 2 minutes. Strain off this water and place the barley in a jug with the thinly pared rind of the lemon, the sugar and the pint of boiling water. Leave till cold then strain, stir in the juice of the lemon and use as required – this is not a drink to store for more than a week.

Mint Drink*

Rather more extravagant but very refreshing.

4 large bunches of fresh mint
2 lb sugar
2 medium (10 oz) bottles dry ginger
juice of 10 lemons or a bottle of unsweetened lemon juice

Wash the mint and break it up. Pour on the sugar and let the mixture stand for 3 to 4 hours for the juices to run. Strain, add the lemon juice and chill. Just before serving pour in the chilled dry ginger.

Rose Hip Syrup

Rose hip syrup is much liked by younger children and is rich in Vitamin C.

1 lb rose hips
2 pints water
¾ lb sugar

Rinse and mince the rose hips and pour on 1½ pints of boiling water. Bring back to the boil then leave to stand in the water for about 15 minutes. Strain the liquid through a double layer of muslin and then return the fruit to the pan, add another ½ pint of boiling water and repeat the process to extract all possible goodness. Mix the two lots of juice together, return to the rinsed pan and boil down to 1 pint. Add the sugar and stir until dissolved. Pour into corked or screw-topped bottles and stand *on* something in a large saucepan. Fill the pan with warm water, bring to the boil and simmer for about 20 minutes.

The syrup made like this should not be diluted but served

neat in little wine glasses. To make a syrup that you can dilute add another ½ lb sugar.

Either version will keep for months in a cool place, but once opened should be used in a week.

Cherry Ice Cubes*

Add these to any cold fruit drinks. Put different coloured glacé cherries (they are available yellow and green as well as red) into each division of the ice tray before topping up with water and freezing. You can do the same thing with sections of mandarin orange or any other neat colourful fruit.

Ices

Any domestic refrigerator enables you to make your own ices and you will find them much more rewarding and much less expensive than any you can buy.

Blackberry Water Ice*

A most popular and unusual ice to try when there are plenty of ripe blackberries. The geranium leaves add a delicious flavour.

1 lb blackberries
¼ lb sugar
¼ pint water
3 sweet-scented geranium leaves

Boil the sugar and water with 2 sweet-scented geranium leaves for 5 minutes. Leave to cool while you sieve the uncooked blackberries. Stir together and pour into the freezing tray of the refrigerator. Place a fresh geranium leaf on top, cover with foil and freeze for about 2½ hours.

Lemon Water Ice

1 pint water
6 oz sugar
3 lemons

Put the rind of the lemons into a saucepan with the water and sugar. Dissolve over low heat then boil rapidly for 5 minutes. Leave to cool then stir in the juice of the lemons and remove the rind. Pour into freezing tray, cover with foil and freeze.

Orange and Lemon Sorbet

Halfway between a water and a cream ice. Strictly speaking a sorbet is less frozen than a water ice and contains a little liqueur.

4 oranges
1 lemon
4 oz sugar
¼ pint water
3 egg whites
¼ pint double cream

Put the sugar and water into a saucepan and grate in the rind of 1 orange and of the lemon. Boil to a thin syrup and leave to cool before mixing with the juice of the oranges and the lemon. Pour into the freezing tray of the refrigerator, cover with foil and put into the freezing compartment for about 2 hours. Turn the frozen mixture out into a bowl. Break it up with a fork into a snow and then quickly mix in the stiffly whisked egg whites and the cream. Re-freeze for about 1 hour. Looks pretty served in the shells of the oranges.

Vanilla Ice Cream

This is a basic -- and quite economical – ice cream recipe which you can vary by adding coffee, melted chocolate, fresh or tinned fruits, nuts, jam, crystallized ginger, glacé fruits, etc.

2 eggs
4 oz caster sugar
½ oz cornflour
1 pint milk
¼ pint double cream
1 teaspoon vanilla essence

Make the custard by whisking together the eggs and the sugar and stirring in the cornflour mixed with a little of the milk. Heat the rest of the milk and add. Return it all to the saucepan, bring to the boil and boil for 3 minutes stirring all the time. Turn into a basin to cool and whisk it now and then to prevent a skin forming. When it is cold pour it into the freezing tray, cover and freeze for about 1½ hours. Turn out and beat well before stirring in the slightly whipped cream flavoured with the vanilla essence. Return to the freezer and freeze for a further hour.

Yogurt

If your children are fond of yogurt this is very much cheaper than buying it ready made and it can be varied by stirring in fruit, nuts, jam and even the leftover syrup from stewed or canned fruit. You only have to buy one small carton of plain yogurt to start you off and from that you can make, in succession, about 6 pints. Get yogurt from a health-food shop if you can.

1 tablespoon plain yogurt
1 pint milk

Boil the milk, pour it into a bowl and let it cool to blood heat then mix one tablespoon of it with the tablespoon of yogurt and stir the resulting cream into the milk. Now keep it warm. Cover the bowl with a plate, wrap it in a towel and leave it in the airing cupboard overnight, when it will be lightly set and can be transferred to the refrigerator to chill. One tablespoon from this brew can be kept back to make the next one but after 5 or 6 rounds it will become too weak and you have to invest in another carton.

Sweetmeats

Home-made sweets are fun to make and can be prettily wrapped up as prizes or leaving presents for parties. Many sweet recipes are rather daunting as they often refer to sugar-boiling thermometers (which few people have) and things like 'small thread', 'small ball' and 'large crack' (which few people understand). Here are some recipes which taste good and which can be made successfully without any particular equipment.

Each recipe will produce about 24 sweets.

Butter Bon-Bons*

4 oz dried milk
2 level tablespoons sugar
1 tablespoon syrup
½ oz butter
almond or vanilla essence

Melt the butter and syrup together then add the sugar and dissolve completely over gentle heat. Add essence to taste and stir in the powdered milk. Mix thoroughly and, while still warm, work with the hands until pliable. Make into long rolls and cut into small, equal-sized pieces. Roll quickly into balls and wrap each in waxed paper.

Chocolate Rum Truffles*

6 oz chocolate
1 egg yolk
1 oz margarine
2 teaspoons rum (or 1 of rum essence)
1 orange
1 teaspoon milk
chocolate vermicelli or hundreds and thousands

Melt the chocolate very gently, beat till smooth and then add the egg yolk, margarine, rum, grated rind of the orange and the milk. Beat until smooth and leave to firm for 5 minutes, then mould into small rounds and toss in chocolate vermicelli or hundreds and thousands. Place in paper sweet cases.

Coconut Pompons*

1 tablespoon honey or redcurrant jelly
1 oz margarine
1 heaped tablespoon icing sugar
4 rounded tablespoons desiccated coconut
glacé cherries

Place the honey or redcurrant jelly in a small bowl. Add the margarine and cream well together, then add the sifted icing sugar and beat well. Stir in the coconut until thoroughly mixed. Form into balls with the palms of the hands and roll in more coconut. Leave to firm on a wire tray then decorate with little bits of glacé cherries and place in paper sweet cases.

Lemon Drops

1½ lb sugar
½ pint water
½ teaspoon cream of tartar
lemon essence
1 dessertspoon tartaric acid
icing sugar

Boil the sugar, water and cream of tartar together until pale yellow. Add the lemon essence to taste and turn out onto an oiled slab. Sprinkle on the tartaric acid and work it well in. As soon as it is cool enough to handle form into thin rolls, cut off short pieces and roll into shape with the hand. Coat with sifted icing sugar and dry well.

Nut Hardbake

1 lb sugar
1 teaspoon cream of tartar
½ pint water
4 oz nuts – chopped

Boil the sugar, water and cream of tartar together until golden. Add the nuts and stir until they too are golden then pour into a greased tin and leave to set.

Peppermint Lumps

2 oz sugar
4 oz syrup
2 oz margarine
4 oz dried milk
3 tablespoons water
peppermint essence

Put the sugar and syrup into a small saucepan with the water and dissolve slowly without stirring. Add the margarine in small knobs, bring to the boil and boil briskly for 8 minutes then stir in the dried milk and peppermint essence. Turn out onto slab and divide into four. When cool enough to handle form into cylinders and cut into lumps with oiled scissors. Wrap in waxed paper.

Chocolate Leaves*

A simple trick which looks expensively professional. Children get great satisfaction from making them and they keep for ages in an airtight tin and always look pretty on cakes, trifles, ices, etc.

All you need is some small leaves (e.g. roses) and some chocolate melted gently in the oven or over a pan of hot water. Wipe the leaves clean with a damp tissue and let them dry thoroughly before towing them, upper side down, over the surface of the melted chocolate. Lay them chocolate side up on a plate and leave in a cool place to set. When they are set firm you will be able to peel the leaf off and will find that the chocolate retains the shape of the leaf and is delicately imprinted with its veins.

Frosted Grapes*

Very sparkly and pretty. Can also be done with cherries or small clusters of red, white or black currants.

Beat the white of an egg to a slight froth and brush over the fruit. Dredge with caster sugar and chill until firm.

Every party goes better with some organized games. I have included proven favourites which you will probably know alongside newer games, and each of the five sections is arranged alphabetically. It is impossible to be dogmatic about the right ages for the games, as groups of children vary a great deal, so treat the ages given only as a rough guide.

1 *Ice Breakers*
2 *Pencil and Paper Games*
3 *Verbal Games*
4 *Strenuous Games*
5 *Magic and Novelties*

8. ICE BREAKERS

Why do many children (and many adults) feel nervous when they actually arrive at a party, although they may well have been looking forward to it? It seems to be a combination of having to confront people they perhaps do not know very well, in clothes which are sometimes formal and uncomfortable, and not knowing quite what is expected of them. Shyness is contagious, so to prevent your party grinding to a halt before it has even got going, launch it with a really good game to break the ice.

Advertisements (age ten upwards)

Rifle old magazines and newspapers for familiar advertisements. Cut them out, but cut off the actual name of the product. Number them and pin them up – well spaced out – around the downstairs rooms and hallway. As the visitors arrive give them each a pencil and post card and ask them to try and name the things advertised. Don't let it drag on too long before checking the lists. It is probably better to avoid giving prizes right at the beginning of the party or some will feel like failures before they have even started.

Autographs (age eight upwards)

Prepare in advance some generous sheets of paper – one for each child – with the names of all the children listed down the left hand side. Hand these out as they arrive (and children are never late for a party – I usually find they all turn up within about four minutes of each other!) and explain that they are to collect the full autograph of each child opposite his name on the list and write their own on other people's lists when requested. The first one to present a complete list is acclaimed the winner but, again, it is better not to bother with a prize at this early stage.

Balloon Throw (ages four to seven)

Even the youngest and most timid guest can cope with this.

Range the children in a line at the edge of the carpet and invite each in turn to throw the balloon as far forward as he can. Mark the farthest throw with a match stick or piece of wool and play several rounds.

Do As I Say (age five upwards)

The children sit in a group facing the leader (probably you). Tell them to concentrate on doing what the leader *says* regardless of what he *does*. When the leader points to his nose and says 'Nose, nose, nose', the children follow suit but if he points to his chin and says 'Ear, ear, ear' then they must point to an ear and not the chin. The first child to make a mistake takes over as leader.

Face to Face (age seven upwards)

The children stand in a circle in pairs facing each other and one child stands in the middle. This child calls out a series of commands such as 'Back to back', 'Side by side', 'On one foot'. When he calls out 'All change', everybody must change partners and the child in the middle must try and secure a partner for himself so that the unlucky one becomes the one in the middle.

Follow my Leader (age four upwards)

This can be a good ice breaker with an imaginative leader – perhaps yourself. It is non-competitive and any inhibitions are quickly forgotten in the general turmoil.

The children simply form a line behind the leader holding onto the waist of the person in front. Everybody imitates the actions of the leader – hopping, jumping, crawling, stretching, scratching, climbing over chairs, under tables, up and down stairs.

Food Hunt (ages six to eight)

Before the children arrive for the party, hide about twenty slips of paper cut from four different coloured sheets.

When they are assembled divide them into four groups and ask each group to appoint a leader. Give each leader a slip of paper in a different colour with DONKEY written on the grey, COW on the brown, DOG on the white, CAT on the orange, etc. Tell the groups that hidden around the house are twenty lots of food for each animal. They must search diligently and when they find a slip of paper – whatever colour it is – they must not touch it but stand near it making the noise of their particular animal until their leader arrives. If it is his colour, he collects it; if it is another colour he crumples it up and puts it in his pocket.

After about ten minutes you call a halt and count the slips. The group with the largest number of slips in their own colour has won.

Getting Knotted (ages six to ten)

Any child whose fingers can manage a simple knot will enjoy this.

You need a ball of leftover knitting wool which you cut into 6″ lengths. Then, with the help of your children, hide these all over the house so that just the very tip is showing. Use a darning needle to pull pieces through curtains, cushion covers, rugs, towels and even the clothes you are wearing!

When the guests have arrived give them each a piece of the wool so that they know what they are looking for and invite them to search the house for more. As soon as they find their second piece they must knot it to their first before they go on looking. The winner is the one who has the longest length either at the end of a set time or when nobody can find any more.

Handshake (age six upwards)

Each child on arrival at the party is given ten dried peas or beans or pebbles. The idea is for them to get rid of these as quickly as they can. This they do by going round the other guests shaking hands with each of them in turn. To every *fifth* person they shake hands with they hand a bean but, of course, as fast as they are unloading them they are getting more back from the other children. It is only with unusual luck or unabashed cheating that anybody will unload their quota – but everyone will unload his shyness by the time you call a halt.

Happy Families   (age eight to ten)

Sort out some Happy Families cards in advance so that if, for instance, you have twelve guests coming you have put aside three families of four persons.

Hand out a card to each child on arrival inviting him to locate the rest of his family (e.g. Mr Bun the Baker, Mrs Bun the Baker's wife, Miss Bun the Baker's daughter and Master Bun the Baker's son). The first family to get together is the winning family and sits down on the floor.

How Do You Do?   (age eight upwards)

Each child is given a number to pin on himself and a pencil and a piece of card with the numbers of all the other guests on it. They have to fill up their cards with the name, age, address and school of each child opposite the number allotted to him. No prizes because the first to arrive will probably be the first to finish, but make a pretence of carefully checking each one. No one can finish until everyone has come so latecomers will find themselves the centre of attention. They won't remember all the names, of course, but the initial strangeness will have evaporated and you always get the jokers who say they are eighty-five and live at the Old Bull and Bush.

Hunt the Pairs (age four upwards)

A very successful ice breaker, especially if you can get your
own children to collect together a whole mass of things (in
pairs) before the party starts. Here are some suggestions:
paperclips, safety pins, dressmaker pins, Smarties – two of
each colour, nuts, dried peas, dried beans, nails, beads,
buttons, matches (used), cocktail sticks, coins, ear-rings,
rubber bands, etc.

Each child is given a small paper bag containing perhaps
six items. The matching pairs will have been hidden all over
the house where they are just partly visible without anything
needing to be moved. The children must hunt around until
they have found the identical pair to the items in their paper
bags. This way they will get used to the house and forget their
strangeness in the excitement.

You can either let them keep their collections or use them
later for a game of memory.

Missing Halves (age six upwards)

Somewhat similar to hunt the pairs, but for this game you
need a bundle of old Christmas cards, birthday cards or post
cards. Cut the cards in half so that the picture is bisected and
hide one half of each anywhere around the ground floor before the children come. As they arrive give them four half
cards each and tell them to search for the matching halves
but to replace any cards they find which do not match. It
is probably best to forget about prizes as the early birds will
again be the winners – perhaps a dip into a box of chocolates
or a tug at a bunch of grapes as they finish is the best solution.

Alternatively you can use a pack of old playing cards. Cut
them into triangles and slide the pieces into hiding places all
over the house. Ask the children to collect as many pieces as
they can find and as they gather you can sneak around
surreptitiously hiding more. After a certain time call a halt

and let them piece together the bits of cards they have. The one with the highest number of complete cards is the winner.

Name Bingo (age eight upwards)

An excellent way of getting the children talking to one another.

Prepare in advance one sheet of stiff paper or card for each child and rule it off into squares – one square for each child present. When they arrive, ask them to write their names first on a slip of paper which they put into a box and then in one of their squares. Now they go round the assembly asking each child his name and filling in the other squares with the names. Don't hurry this part, for the idea, after all, is that they should get to know each other a bit.

Once all the squares are completed everybody sits down and you take the box of slips of paper into your lap. When you read out the first name that child locates himself by standing up and saying 'That's me', and then he and everybody else cross out his name on their charts. You go on reading out the names until someone has a whole line (vertical, horizontal or diagonal) crossed out, when he shouts 'Bingo'.

If you want to play the game several times have some little squares of paper or disks which the children can use to cover the names as they are called and which can be removed at the end.

Nosey Parkers (age seven upwards)

Prepare some stiff cards by ruling out twelve squares on each side. In the corner of each square write a letter of the alphabet (but omit 'q' and 'x'). Hand out a card to each child and ask him to wander wherever he likes in the house and garden writing down everything he can see in the appropriate square (e.g. 'c' square: chair, cushion, cat, candle, carpet, cooker; in the 'd' square: desk, doorknob, door, dustbin, etc.) They must not touch or move anything. Spelling is unimportant. The winner can either be the person who has the most entries or, as in Matchbox Filling (*see* p. 31) you can ask one guest to read out his list while everyone who has the same crosses out that entry. The winner will be the one who has most left when all the lists have been checked off.

Pass the Parcel (age four upwards)

This is a good ice breaker because you don't have to know anybody's name or where anything is kept in a strange house and the children are united by the exciting mystery of the parcel.

Before the party starts select some rather special little gift (suitable for a boy or girl) and wrap it in layers and layers and layers of paper and string so that it ends up much bigger than its original size.

You need a record player, radio or piano. Range the children in a circle and get them to pass the parcel from one to the other as long as the music is playing. As soon as it stops the child who is holding the parcel unwraps one layer and then passes it on until the secret is revealed. The lucky one who removes the last piece of paper is the winner and keeps the present.

It's a good idea to have a large cardboard box in the middle to receive the paper as it is torn off.

Puzzle Boxes (age nine upwards)

Prepare ten or twelve matchboxes by filling them each with one of a variety of things such as used matches, sugar, sultanas, pins, dried peas, rice, sand, crisps, bath crystals, pebbles, nails, beads, etc. Number each matchbox clearly on both sides, seal them and range them on a large table.

As the children arrive hand them each a pencil and a post card with the numbers of the matchboxes written down the left hand side. Ask them to try and guess by noise, weight and smell what each matchbox contains and to write their guess down opposite the appropriate number. Heated discussion will ensue and shyness will be forgotten.

You can also do the same sort of thing with little muslin bags hung on a 'clothes line' containing different smelly things like coffee, cinnamon, curry powder, pepper, cloves, etc. (This version is often called Chinese Laundry.)

Ring of Roses (age three to six)

Most tiny children are familiar with this. Curiously enough it has a somewhat sinister history, as it is supposed to date from the time of the Great Plague, the first symptom being sneezing after which you fell down dead! The words are:

> Ring a ring of roses
> A pocketful of posies.
> Tish – oo! Tish – oo!
> All fall down.

The children join hands and dance around in a circle singing and at the words 'Tish – oo' they 'all fall down.'

After a few straight rounds you can make it more competitive by deciding that the last to fall down shall be eliminated.

Word Objects (age nine upwards)

Play this only with a small and docile group. Divide the children into pairs. One of each pair thinks of a short word and collects objects from his pockets or about the room. The first letters of these objects will form the word. He might get a paper, an orange and a teapot to form 'pot' or a cushion, an apple and a pin to form 'cap'. It makes it too easy to arrange the objects in the right order and it is more fun for the other child if they are shuffled around.

Objects should be replaced after each word and partners changed after about five minutes.

Word Pairs (age eight to ten)

Give each child three bits of paper on which you have written a word like 'some', 'any', 'every', 'thing', 'body', 'time', etc., each of which will combine in different ways to form various longer words. Tell each child to find a partner whose word will combine with one of his to form another word and then keep this partner for the following games.

9. PENCIL AND PAPER GAMES

At some stage in most parties it is good to have the children quietly occupied with pencils and paper. For the majority of these games the children have to be able to write, but some require only rudimentary drawing.

Beetle (age seven upwards)

This is the game that we called 'Hangman' when I was a child.

Divide the children into groups of four or six – with larger groupings they get bored awaiting their turn. Each group needs a big sheet of paper and must choose one player to start.

This player selects a longish word (e.g. buttercup) which he keeps secret. He then puts on the paper a dash for each letter in the word and writes all the letters of the alphabet down the side. The other children take it in turns to suggest a letter. The leader immediately crosses it off in the alphabet list. If it *is* in his word, he writes it in on the appropriate dash; if it is *not* in the word, he starts to draw the beetle – the body for the first wrong letter, then the head, then one feeler, then the other, then each of the four legs in turn for each wrong letter that is suggested. (For this game beetles have only four legs or you'll never get the children home to bed.) Whoever guesses or completes the word correctly chooses the next one; but if the beetle is complete before the word then the same child chooses another word.

The group with the lowest number of completed beetles is the winning group.

Blindfold Drawing (age five upwards)

Spread a large sheet of paper on a table and ask for a volunteer to be your artist. Blindfold him and give him a fat crayon or felt-tip pen. Then ask him to draw a house (or a horse or a car or a person – or perhaps something that he suggests because it is a speciality), but he must do it step by step as the other children tell him: 'First do the roof.' 'Now do the door.' 'Now do an upstairs window.'

The children watching will gain much amusement from the chaotic results – as will the artist himself when he sees them!

Consequences (age ten upwards)

A very old favourite.

Give out pencils and paper and seat the children in a circle. At the top of their paper ask them to write the name of a man or boy, fold the paper over once and and pass it to the person on their left. It is more amusing if the people named are known by everybody either personally or through some claim to fame. Then they all write the name of a woman or girl, fold and hand it on. Next comes 'Where they met', then 'What he said to her', 'What she said to him' and finally 'The consequences were . . .'

When the consequences are completed, the papers are folded, again handed to the left and each child reads out the paper with which he ends up.

Crossword (age nine upwards)

Each child has a pencil and paper and draws four lines crossing to form nine squares: three rows of three. The children take it in turns to call out a letter and, as each letter is called, all the children must write it into one of their squares. The idea is to form as many words vertically or horizontally as possible. The same letter may be called out more than once if somebody needs it to form a word. When nine letters have been called, score three points for three-letter words and two points for two-letter words.

Draw the Tail (age five upwards)

Similar to the classic pinning the tail on the donkey.

Draw some large animal (real or imaginary) on a sheet of wrapping paper or the back of some leftover wallpaper with a thick black crayon or felt pen. Give a different coloured felt pen or crayon to each child. Place your drawing on a table (safer than the wall which over-enthusiastic guests may draw on by mistake), blindfold the children in turn and invite them to draw on the tail where they think it ought to be. The tail which comes nearest to your original black one is the winner.

Fishing (age seven upwards)

Divide a large sheet of paper into nine squares and, with the help of the children, write in each square a proper name or the name of an animal, town or flower.

Place the paper on a table and invite the children to stand around and study it for a few minutes to try and memorize which name is where. Then blindfold one child and give him a pencil. The child on his right chooses a name and asks him to make a stab with the pencil at what he thinks is the position of that name. If the pencil mark misses, he falls out but, if it is within the right square, he moves to the end to await his next turn and so on until you are left with an outright winner.

Freaky Figures (age eight upwards)

This is a pictorial version of consequences.

The children sit in a circle with a pencil and paper each. They start by drawing a head – human or animal – at the top of the paper and then folding the paper so that just the end of the neck is visible. They each hand their paper to the left and then draw a body on the paper they receive leaving lines below the fold to indicate where the legs are attached – and so on.

The unfolding causes much hilarity.

Journalism (age ten upwards)

Each child has a piece of paper and a pencil and is asked to write a question – as serious or as silly as he chooses – at the top of the paper, fold it over and pass it on to the next child. Next they write any word they like on the folded paper, but preferably a fairly difficult or unusual word, and pass it on again. Now everybody opens the paper they have received and has to compose a sentence which will answer the question and somehow include the word. Can be quite difficult and very amusing.

Letter Puzzle (age ten upwards)

Each child in turn calls out a letter of the alphabet and all the children write them down in the same order.

They must then each try to construct a sentence in which the words will start with the letters given, in the order in which they were called out, e.g.

a	f	h	w	p	i	t	m
a	fat	hen	waddled	proudly	in the mud;		
another	foolish	hat	was	purchased	in the market.		

Additional letters can be used, but the best sentence will be judged on its sense and the minimum of additions.

Listening (age eight upwards)

A wonderful game when you desperately need a few quiet moments.

Give each child pencil and paper and ask them to write down every sound they hear in the next five minutes – the more minute and almost inaudible the better. It demands concentration and some degree of imagination and, apart from the obvious ones which they'll all get like cars, motor-bikes or aircraft passing, car doors banging, birdsong, some-one coughing, a baby crying, passers-by talking, there are also a whole host of things like Jon's pencil squeaking, Jane's paper rustling, Tom's shoe scraping, a tap dripping, leaves blowing, someone breathing, tummy rumbling and a brace-let tinkling.

The child with the longest list is the winner and it's a game worth repeating later in the party as subsequent rounds get increasingly subtle.

Memory (age eight upwards)

Prepare a large trayful of tiny objects such as a button, a sweet, a drawing pin, string, a potato, a match, a thimble, and so on. Put the tray down in the middle of the floor and tell the children to study it hard. Then remove it and ask them to write down as many articles as they can remember. It helps to tell them how many different things there were. After five or ten minutes stop them and ask the youngest to read out his list. As each item is read out the others who have got it cross that one out and then they are asked in turn if they have any others. The one with the longest correct list deserves a small prize.

Missing Letters (age seven upwards)

Prepare a slip of paper for each child on which you have printed the same ten words with some of the letters missing, e.g. 'r – – b – t', 'bl – e – e – l', ' – ig – – n'. The length and difficulty of the words will depend on your age group. Give a folded slip to each child and at the word 'Go' let them try to complete the words. When someone calls out 'Finished', everyone stops while you check the completed list. If it is correct, this child is the winner. If not, say 'Go' again and let the others resume.

Nature Guess (age nine upwards)

Peaceful and instructive.

Before the party ask your children to collect together a boxful of flowers (with well defined petals), seed pods, ears of corn, twigs bearing berries, ferns, sprays of leaves, etc. – one item for each child present or two if your group is very small. Attach a number to each with a wisp of Sellotape.

Give the children pencils and paper, hold up the items in

turn for a couple of seconds and ask them to write down its number and to guess at the number of petals or seeds or berries or leaves on each one.

Once you have held them all up in turn, hand them out for the children to do the actual counting and then you can check the lists. If nobody gets any of them absolutely right, award one point to whoever guessed the nearest in each case.

Never Heard Anything Like It (age seven upwards)

Before the party make a list of noises you can make and assemble the properties necessary. You could make the following noises: squeaking a balloon; snapping fingers; dropping pins; brushing hair; brushing a skirt; spraying aerosol; tearing cloth; tearing paper; bouncing a ball; striking a match; winding a watch; syphoning soda; bursting a paper bag; knitting; sharpening a pencil; closing a book, etc.

Give each child a pencil and paper and retire behind a curtain or screen telling the children to sit in deathly silence and listen. After each noise they write down what they think it was and at the end you check the lists.

Person, Place and Thing (age ten upwards)

Choose a short word such as 'life', 'band', 'chop', and ask the children to print it vertically down the left hand side of their paper. Now decide between you on the sorts of persons, places and things you want to select. (It could be famous Englishmen, sportsmen or pop stars, and towns or countries and food, machines or domestic objects.)

Once these are settled the children can start filling in their papers, e.g.

	Person	Place	Thing
C	Churchill	Coventry	Carpet
H	Hornblower	Hull	Hoover
O	Oates	Oldham	Opener
P	Prince Philip	Portsmouth	Pan

The first one to complete a correct list is the winner.

Picture Guessing (age seven upwards)

Divide the children into two teams and provide a piece of paper and a pencil for each.

The first team must decide on the title of a TV programme, a book or a song. They write this down (so that the other team won't hear it) and hand it to the leader of the second team.

The leader goes back to his team and, without speaking, tries to draw pictures which will give the other children clues to the title. Whether it is 'Goldilocks' or 'Goldfinger' will depend on the age, tastes and sophistication of the groups involved.

If the second team guesses correctly, it is their turn to choose a subject. If they give up, the first team chooses again but a different child from the second team acts as artist.

Sweet Guesses (age seven upwards)

Stage this early on in the party – certainly not after tea – and keep the portions absolutely minuscule.

The children must be blindfolded and you have to prepare a bowl or a plate with a slightly raised rim for each one holding, for example: a peanut, a sultana, a square of chocolate, a cashew, a tangerine segment, a grape, a crisp, a minute cube of cheese, half a glacé cherry, a cornflake.

The children are told that there are ten items on their plates which they must eat, try to identify and try to remember.

When everyone has munched their way through their assortment, blindfolds are removed and each tries to write down what he has eaten. The one with most right is the winner.

Triplets (age nine upwards)

Give each child three slips of paper and ask them to write a different word on each, fold them over and place them all in a basket.

Shuffle them then pass the basket round and ask each player to take out three slips and compose a sentence using those three words. Alternate rounds could be funny or sensible sentences.

Vocabulary Test (age seven upwards)

Pick a subject such as animals, boys' names, girls' names, flowers, trees, towns, etc. and ask the children to write down as many of them as they can in three minutes. The player with the longest correct list is the winner.

Word Making (age nine upwards)

This is a classic which always ensures a few quiet minutes.

Hand out pencils and paper and give the children a long word to print at the top of their paper. Choose a word with two or three vowels and a variety of consonants (e.g. understand, tremendous, combination, Australian, impersonate). Tell them to rearrange the letters to form as many smaller words as they can in ten minutes. They then read out their lists in turn and each legitimate word scores one point – adding 's' does *not* score another point. A prize for the highest number of points.

You can vary this by giving the children a proverb, quotation or short sentence with which to do the same thing.

10. VERBAL GAMES

Since they demand absolutely no equipment, a stock of good verbal games is always useful – not only for parties but on journeys, picnics or when the children are ill.

Alphabetitis (ages six to nine)

A good exercise for children who are still fairly new to the alphabet.

Point to any of the children and call out a word for them to spell. Of course you must tailor your choice to suit the reading age of the children present. If you call out 'cricket' the child must spell the word but then continue: 'uvwxyz' – after the last letter up to the end of the alphabet. You can make the game competitive or simply educational depending on the group.

Alphabet Objects   (age nine upwards)

The first child to spot an object in the room or visible through the window which begins with the letter 'a' says: 'I see something beginning with "a" and it's an apple.'

The child next to him looks for something beginning with 'b' and follows suit. Anyone who is stumped falls out and, if everyone is stumped by a letter, then skip it and carry on.

Animal, Vegetable or Mineral   (age ten upwards)

Give one child a bean bag, small cushion or a nut – something he can throw to another child without risk. As he throws he calls out either 'animal', 'vegetable' or 'mineral' and then starts counting. The child who is catching must respond by calling out an example of an animal, a vegetable or a mineral before the first child has counted up to ten. If he succeeds, it is his turn to make a throw and choose the category; if he fails, he falls out and the first child throws again.

Bang   (age nine upwards)

Bang is fun and calls for quick thinking.

Choose one child to start. He points to one of the children and calls out a three-letter word such as 'pot'. He then counts up to ten and says 'Bang'. The other child must name three objects beginning with the three letters in pot e.g. pea, orange, towel. If he fails to do this before the first child says 'Bang', he must be the next Banger.

Betty's Apples (age ten upwards)

Children who have had to wrestle with intelligence tests in school will soon get the hang of this.

For the first couple of rounds be the Question Master yourself and, if they haven't broken the code, help them to analyse why one answer was right and another was wrong.

You could start off with:

'Betty likes apples but hates pears. What do you like?'

If the child answers:

'I like bananas,' you reply,

'I'm sorry. You didn't get the message. Billy likes running but hates walking. What do you like?'

If the child answers:

'I like swimming,' you can say:

'You may send the answering message,' for the secret of the code is the double letter in the *subject* and the *object* of the sentence: Be*tt*y – a*pp*les, Bi*ll*y – ru*nn*ing. So the child who has mastered it can go on with Jenny likes kittens, puppies like slippers, etc.

When most of the children have got it, change the code, e.g. Ro*y* likes jell*y*, Ro*ger* likes gin*ger* and so on.

Bung Ho! (age five upwards)

An unusual game which can be very funny. Basically all you need is one cork but I suppose our highly-tuned hygienic consciences would be happier if there were several, floating, between turns, in a bowl of slightly salted water.

The children are divided into two teams and sit opposite each other. One team decides on a question. The first child places a cork between his teeth and speaks the question to the other team. His tongue must not touch the cork, but he can – and will have to – repeat the question as often as requested.

When the other team finally understands and answers the

question correctly it is their turn to choose a question, a spokesman and a cork.

Just *try* saying 'Who is the Prime Minister of Britain?' or 'Where does the sun rise and set?' with a cork between your teeth!

Ghost (age ten upwards)

The children take it in turns to call out letters but the aim is *not* to be the one who calls a letter that completes a word.

The first child might say 'p' and the second might say 'a'. Now the third child must avoid saying 'n' or 't' or 'y' all of which would complete a word but must try and think of a longer word ('painting', 'pastime', 'passport', 'pause') and say the next letter of that.

If he cannot, he loses the first of his five chances and is dubbed a 'g', then 'gh', 'gho', 'ghos', 'ghost' – when he's out.

If he says something wildly suspect like 'q' or 'z', anybody can challenge him and ask him what word he is thinking of. Bluffing will cost him another of his chances and the challenger starts a new word.

Happy Birthday (age six upwards)

The children sit in a circle with one in the middle, who moves around and suddenly points to one child, saying 'Happy Birthday to you'. While he is saying this, the child to whom he is pointing must reply 'The same to you' *before* the first one has finished.

If, however, the child in the centre just points without speaking, the child he is pointing at must say nothing. If he is too hasty and starts to speak, he becomes the one in the middle.

I'm Thinking of a Colour   (age six upwards)

One child selects an object and says to the others:

'I'm thinking of something you can see and it is green,' without, of course, looking at the object.

The other children then take it in turns to ask questions which the first child must only answer with yes or no. If the answer is yes the questioner can continue until he gets a no when the next child takes up the questions. Whoever guesses the object chooses the next one.

The children will soon get the idea of not asking questions that are too specific so that they go on getting yes answers. For instance, instead of saying 'Is it Sara's dress?' they might say 'Is it someting to wear?' and go on from there.

I Spy   (age six upwards)

This is so well known that it needs no explanation but do not underestimate its gap-filling potential.

Start it off by saying:

'I spy with my little eye something beginning with "c".' The children will then fire questions at you – 'Is it the curtains?' 'Is it the carpet?' 'Is it the cushion?' – and the one who gets it right chooses the next I spy.

The game may be varied by describing characteristic features of an object and not giving its first letter, for instance:

'I spy something which is soft and red' (a cushion) or 'I spy something round and green' (an apple).

Last Letter   (age eight upwards)

A test of spelling and quick thinking. One child starts by calling out a word and then spelling it. While spelling it he points to another child, who has to say a word beginning with the last letter and then spell that.

The first child who fails to think of a sequel or to spell it correctly falls out.

Letter Cards   (age nine upwards)

If you have a set of cards or counters bearing the letters of the alphabet (e.g. Lexicon or Scrabble), these will serve very well for letter cards. Otherwise cut out some squares of cardboard and make your own.

Spread out all the letters face downwards on table or floor. The first child picks one up at random, calls out what it is and places it face upwards in front of him while everyone tries to think of an animal or a town or a fruit or flower – whatever subject you have settled on – which begins with that letter. The first one to sing out an answer is given the letter and has the privilege of turning over the next. The winner is the child who has the largest number of letters at the end.

Link Names   (age nine upwards)

A good game for both spelling and geography.

The first child says the name of a town, e.g. London. The second child has to respond with another town beginning with the last letter of the first, e.g. Norwich, and so on. Anyone who can't follow on falls out and the next child starts a new series. Wiley ones will soon realize that towns ending in 'e' or 'y' tend to stump people as, apart from Exeter, Edinburgh and Eastbourne or Yeovil and Ypres, there aren't many that they know.

You can also play this game with Christian names.

Menu Making   (age eight upwards)

A real vocabulary tester and memory twister.

The first child starts off the game by saying:

'For dinner today I had some apples.'

The second child takes it up with:

'For dinner today I had some apples and some black-berries,' and so on through the alphabet.

Any player who cannot think of an item to add or who repeats the menu incorrectly falls out.

Old Mother Hubbard   (ages five to eight)

One of those mad games that can be fun once in a while.

The first child turns to the child on his left and says: 'Old Mother Hubbard is coming to stay.'

'What is she like?' asks the second child.

'She has her mouth wide open,' the first child replies and then sits with his mouth wide open while the second child passes it on by the same routine, until everyone is sitting with their mouths wide open.

In the next round another peculiar characteristic is added, such as:

'She always has her legs crossed,' or

'She always has her arms folded,' until the whole group is a most extraordinary sight. *But* smiling and giggling at Old Mother Hubbard's eccentricities are strictly forbidden and anyone who weakens has to fall out.

Sam Smith's Suitcase   (ages seven to nine)

A mildly challenging game to get the children thinking.

Start by saying:

'My name is Sam Smith. I'm going on holiday so I've got to pack my suitcase. I'll take some of you with me if you tell me the right things to pack. Remember – I'm *S*am *S*mith and I'm packing a *s*uitcase.'

The children then take it in turns to say what they would pack. If the first child says:

'My name is Jane and I shall pack a swimsuit,' Mr Smith replies:

'I'm sorry but you'll have to stay at home this time.'
If the second child says:
'My name is Paul and I shall pack some pencils,' Mr Smith says: 'Right – you can come,' because Paul has packed something beginning with the same letter as his name. Play several rounds, so that those who missed out the first time can have more chances.

Simon Says   (age four upwards)

This is an old favourite which can help increase vocabulary and speed reactions.

Start off by leading yourself. Stand in front of the children and issue a series of commands all preceded by 'Simon says', e.g. 'Simon says hands on your head. Simon says fold your arms. Simon says open your mouth.' When you give a command which does *not* begin with 'Simon says' the children must ignore it and anyone who inadvertently obeys falls out.

If the group is standing, you have more scope, for they can hop, squat, kneel, touch toes, etc. Older children can try it in elementary French or German or whatever they are learning at school.

Tail Ender   (age ten upwards)

The children are seated in a circle and one starts by saying a two-syllable word (e.g. pavement). The next player takes the second syllable and adds another to form a new two-syllable word (e.g. mental), *but* he must think carefully, for each final syllable must be usable as the first of a new word (e.g. al-so, sof-ten, ten-der). A bluffer can be challenged and must fall out. Having a dictionary at hand helps.

Teapot   (age nine to eleven)

Divide the children into two groups and have one group

leave the room while the other decides on a verb such as 'walk'. The first group returns and interrogates the others, asking questions which can only be answered by 'yes' or 'no', e.g.

'Do children teapot?' 'Yes.'
'Do fish teapot?' 'No.'
'Do you like to teapot?' 'Yes.'
'Do you teapot often?' 'Yes.'
'Do you teapot outside?' 'Yes.'

and so on until the verb is discovered.

The Thomases' Cat (age seven upwards)

This is also known as The Curate's Cat, but of course you can claim ownership as you like. Arrange the children in a circle and pick the youngest one to start the game off. The idea is to go through the alphabet finding different adjectives to describe the cat, e.g.

The Thomases' cat is an *a*ngry cat.
The Thomases' cat is a *b*lack cat.
The Thomases' cat is a *c*uddly cat.

Tommy Tommy (age five upwards)

Invite the children to watch you closely. Point with the index finger of your left hand to the little finger of your right and then to each finger in turn, saying: 'Tommy, Tommy, Tommy, Tommy, Whoops, Tommy.'

You say 'Whoops' as you slide down the first finger of the right hand then up your thumb. Repeat the action in the opposite direction starting with the thumb and saying: 'Tommy, Whoops, Tommy, Tommy, Tommy, Tommy.' Then fold your arms and invite any child to imitate exactly what you have done. The point is that after doing all the finger business correctly and getting the words right they must *fold their arms* as you have done.

You can vary it by clearing your throat before you start or scratching your head or crossing your legs; see how long it takes them all to catch on.

Touch Shopping (age nine upwards)

The children sit in a circle and the first child says to the child on his left:

'I've been shopping today.'

'What did you buy?' asks the second.

'A dress,' replies the first without explanation.

The second child then turns to his neighbour and says he too has been shopping. It is not necessary to explain this at the outset, but the children are in fact only allowed to buy things which they could actually *touch* from where they sit. If some-one says:

'I've been shopping and I bought a car,' you must say 'No' and help them all to decide what it is that makes some things eligible and some not. Once the principle is established the game can go on for quite a long time providing you let them sit in different places in the room.

What Can I Buy? (age seven upwards)

The children sit in a circle with one in the centre who is the 'buyer'. The buyer says:

'I'm going to London. What should I buy there?' He then points to one of the children and begins to count to ten. The other child must reply with two things beginning with the same letter as the town (e.g. lace and linen) and, if he fails to do this before the count of ten, he becomes the buyer.

Whispering (age seven upwards)

Seat the children in a circle or, if you have more than ten, make two teams.

Write down a fairly complicated sentence on a slip of paper, fold it over and hand it to the first child, at the same time whispering the sentence to him or her. Without looking at the paper he must repeat exactly what he thinks he has heard – even though it may seem to make no sense – to the next child and pass the paper on. No one must open the paper but, when the message gets to the last child, he speaks it aloud and then reads out the message on the paper. The discrepancy between the two will cause much hilarity. (The classic, of course, is 'Send reinforcements we're going to advance,' which became 'Send three and fourpence we're going to a dance'!)

Who Am I? (age eight upwards)

Somebody chooses a famous personality and the other children in turn ask questions to which he may only answer 'Yes' or 'No'. For example:
'Are you a man?'
'Are you alive?'
'Are you British?'
'Are you an entertainer?'
Anybody who thinks he has the answer can call it out and if he is right becomes the next personality.

Word Spinning (age nine upwards)

Points are scored here for quick thinking and wide vocabulary.

You need a stop watch (or a watch with a seconds hand) and the letters of the alphabet on cards or counters – omitting 'j', 'k', 'q', 'v', 'x', and 'z'.

Put the letters into a bowl, divide the players into two teams and station yourself by the bowl with the watch. The first player from one team takes a letter and sings out as many words beginning with that particular letter he can think of in half a minute. Make a note of the total.

The first player in the other team then picks out a letter and so on until all twenty letters have been used up. The team with the highest total is the winner.

Yes and No (age seven upwards)

To start this you will need a smooth-talking, quick-thinking character.

The idea is for one child to fire a volley of questions at another child with the object of trying to get him to answer 'Yes' or 'No' – which the victim must resolutely avoid. For example:

'How old are you?'
'I'm eight.'
'*Eight*?'
'That's right.'
'I thought you said six.'
'No – oops!' When someone slips up, he becomes the question master. If they get too good at avoiding 'Yes' and 'No', make 'I' the forbidden word – even more difficult.

11. STRENUOUS GAMES

To work off excess energy and to furnish some organized excitement.

All Change (age five upwards)

Suitable for indoors or out. All the players sit on chairs, stools or cushions in a circle, except for one who stands in the middle. He calls out which players are to change places and, while they are doing so, he tries to slip into one of their places. If he succeeds, the child who has lost his place stays in the middle.

The child in the middle can either pick two or more people by name or by group. For example, he could say:
'All change those with white socks on.'
'All change those who like jelly.'
'All change those with blue eyes.'

Ankle Race   (age five upwards)

Divide the children into pairs and have them race each other from one end of the garden to the other grasping an ankle in each hand all the way. The winners of each pair can go into the second round and race against one another until you are left with one outright winner.

Balloon Race   (age four upwards)

This may be played in a large room or outside if it is not too windy.

You need a balloon and a short stick for each child and one large cardboard box or tea chest. If you consider that sticks could be dangerous, the children can use their hands. Have some extra balloons ready blown up in reserve.

Start the children as far away from the box as space permits. The idea is to persuade the balloons towards and into the box using only the stick or the palm of one hand.

Blindman's Buff   (ages five to nine)

An all-time favourite with younger children but one which you should supervise closely. Be sure to remove any low objects which could trip children up and stow away things with sharp edges and hard corners. It is really better played indoors, as open spaces make it too easy to evade the blindman and he can blunder on for ages without a catch.

One child is blindfolded and moves around twisting and

turning suddenly with arms outstretched trying to catch one of the other children. When he succeeds he must guess who it is – either from the child's giggles or from what he is wearing – and if he is right, the victim becomes the blindman.

Bowling   (age five upwards)

You can play this outside with lawn tennis balls or inside with table tennis balls.

The children are divided into two teams and take it in turns to try and roll the balls into a large box placed on its side either from the far end of the lawn or from the opposite side of the room.

The team which scores the most successes is the winner.

Cat and Mouse   (ages four to seven)

The children stand in a circle holding hands while one volunteer (the mouse) stands in the centre and another (the cat) on the outside.

The idea is for the cat to try and catch the mouse but whereas the mouse is free to go in and out of the children as he pleases, the cat must follow his route and only go through the ring of children where he does. The children in the circle assist the mouse by raising their arms to let him through but are allowed to lower them if they want to in order to make life more difficult for the cat.

If the cat succeeds in catching the mouse, ask for two more volunteers and, if the chase seems too uneven, change the protagonists after a few minutes.

Catch the Plate   (age six upwards)

The children sit cross-legged on the floor in a circle. One stands in the centre with a round wooden bread board or tin plate which won't break. He stands it on edge and spins it, calling out the name of another child who must dash forward and try and catch it before it spins to a standstill flat on the ground. If he succeeds he is the next spinner.

Every now and then you will have to widen the circle and get everyone sitting cross-legged again as, in the general excitement, they get on to their feet or knees and move in closer and closer.

Catch Who Can (age six upwards)

This is similar to catch the plate but a large ball or balloon is used instead. The children stand in a circle and the one in the centre throws the ball high in the air, calling out the name of one of the children, who has to catch it before it falls to the ground. If he succeeds, he throws the ball up; if he fails, the first child has another turn.

Donkey (age six upwards)

You can play this indoors with a light plastic ball or outdoors with a slightly heavier ball.

Get the children to stand in a circle and you stand in the centre. Throw the ball to them one after another. Keep throwing to different parts of the circle, so that they are all kept alert. Anyone who misses it drops down on one knee. If he catches his next throw he can get up again but if he misses a second time he has to go down on two knees, then sit, then lie and, if he misses it when lying down, he is disqualified.

As the game progresses and the better catchers are left, you can increase the speed and force of your delivery to get them out.

Giant Step (age five upwards)

A well-worn classic also called Grandmother's footsteps. It is better played outdoors, but can be played in a biggish room if you don't object to the children scampering back to base.

The children stand behind a line at one end of the garden and one child stands at the far end with his back to them. While the leader's back is turned the children cautiously move forward a little bit but if any of them is caught moving or even wobbling when the leader whips around, they are sent back to the starting line. Each time that the leader turns his back they advance a little further until one is close enough to touch him. If he can manage to touch the leader and race back to base without being caught, he is the winner and takes over as leader.

I Wrote a Letter   (ages four to seven)

The children are seated in a circle and one child is chosen and given a letter. He skips around the outside of the circle while the others chant or sing:

> I wrote a letter to my love,
> And on the way I dropped it.
> One of you has picked it up,
> And put it in her pocket.

The child with the letter drops it behind one of the other children who picks it up and chases him to try and give the letter back to him before the first child steals his place in the circle. If he succeeds, the first child has to have another turn at unloading the letter but if he fails, he becomes the next dropper.

Jumble Sale   (age four upwards)

Collect together a large assortment of funny old clothes – hats, boots, jackets, skirts, aprons, etc. If there are twelve children you will need thirty items.

Put ten of these on a table or in a pile at the far end of the room or garden where you are playing. The children sit in a line at the opposite end and, when you say 'Go', they *hop* to the clothes, grab something, put it on and hop back to their places. The two who have nothing fall out and can help you sort out eight more items for the next round – then six, then four, then two. They keep on the clothes from each round so that they end up looking like scarecrows.

Prizes for the last two, and they usually want to start all over again.

Jumping in the River   (age five upwards)

A little game useful for filling gaps.

Line up the children about 4' apart in two rows facing each other. When you call out 'In the river', they all jump forward and, when you call 'On the bank', they all jump back but, if you say '*In* the bank' or '*On* the river', they must stand fast and anyone who moves or wobbles is disqualified.

Knock It Off   (age six upwards)

Give each child two dessertspoons. In the right hand spoon place an onion, a potato or a ping pong ball. The idea is for the children to race about, keeping their right spoon filled but using their left hand spoon to try and dislodge the other children's onions (or potatoes or balls). This can either be a free-for-all or you can have heats in pairs and let the winners play each other.

Lemon Golf   (age five upwards)

A walking stick, a plastic lemon half filled with water and a series of 'obstacles' consisting of gateways made of books, plastic bottles or skittles are needed for this game which can be played on an intensive indoor circuit or a more extensive outdoor one.

The aim of the game is to manoeuvre the lemon from one end of the course to the other using only the end of the walking stick. The children take it in turn to tee off while the others act as gleeful referees, penalizing him with one point each time he touches an obstacle either with the lemon or with the stick. The one with the fewest penalties is the winner.

Mini Golf (age six upwards)

Mark out two lines at opposite ends of the lawn or carpet and marshal the children in two teams behind them.

Give the first child in each team a tennis ball and invite them to propel it using only the matchstick provided across to the far line and back again before handing over to the next child in the team. Anyone who touches the ball with hands or feet must go back to the line and start again.

You can make it more difficult by rigging up hoops, slopes, parallel lines through which the balls have to pass.

Musical Chairs (age six upwards)

This of course is an old favourite but always popular. You will need a record player, radio or piano to provide the music.

Get enough chairs for all but one of the children and line them up facing alternate ways down the centre of the room. When the music starts, the children march around the room as far away from the chairs as space permits. As soon as the music stops they make a dash for the chairs and the child who fails to get one falls out. One chair is subtracted and the game is resumed until there is an outright winner.

Musical Scramble (ages five to ten)

Somewhat similar to musical chairs, this also requires record player, radio or piano to provide intermittent music.

In the centre of the play space put a tray bearing an assortment of small objects – cotton reels, nuts, buttons, beads, shells – but have one fewer objects than there are children. Range the children as far away from the tray as possible. When the music starts, they must hop or jump round in a circle and when it stops they race to the tray and try to grab an object. The child who is without one falls out and the rest replace their objects (one of which you extract each time) and start again when the music resumes. It is advisable to place the tray on a low table or upturned box so that not so many heads crack together as everyone dives simultaneously.

Necklaces   (ages six to ten)

For twelve children prepare six saucers each holding ten beads or buttons, six lengths of thread heavily knotted at one end and six large, blunt bodkins.

Put the beads at one end of the room or garden and the bodkins and thread at the far end. Divide the children into pairs and start them all off at the thread end. They must decide which of them is going to be the runner and which the threader. At the word 'Go' the threader starts to thread the bodkin and the runner runs to the saucer, picks out two beads and races back with them. The threader then takes them from her and threads them while the runner races for two more. The first pair to complete and tie on their necklace are the winners.

For very young children use string and big wooden beads or big buttons.

Oranges and Lemons   (ages four to six)
Here are the words:

> Oranges and lemons,
> Say the bells of St Clement's.
> You owe me five farthings,
> Say the bells of St Martin's.

When will you pay me?
Say the bells of Old Bailey.
When I grow rich,
Say the bells of Shoreditch.
When will that be?
Say the bells of Stepney.
I'm sure I don't know,
Says the great bell of Bow.
Here comes a candle to light you to bed.
Here comes a chopper to chop off your head.

Choose two of the children to be Orange and Lemon and have them stand facing each other with their clasped hands held up to form an archway. The other children then form a line holding onto the waist of the child in front. They run underneath the arch while everybody sings the song, then circle Orange, go under the arch again and circle Lemon. The last two lines are sung by Orange and Lemon in a menacing manner and at the word 'head' they drop their arms over whichever child is passing through the arch at the time. The victim then chooses whether she wants to be an orange or a lemon and stands behind her choice holding on to her waist and so on until all the children are sorted out. The game ends with a tug-of-war between the two factions.

Over the River   (age five upwards)

Make a 'river' by stretching out two long lengths of string or wool fairly close together at one end and getting progressively wider apart.

The children take it in turns to try a standing-jump across, starting at the narrow end. If they succeed they do a standing-jump back again, but if they get their feet wet they must drop out and go back to the end of the queue.

The winner is the one who jumps the widest part of the river without getting his feet wet.

Peanut Race (age five upwards)

Divide the children into four groups and have two groups at each end of the garden. Place a bowl before each group – two empty at one end of the garden and two containing a teaspoon and three peanuts at the other.

At the word 'Go' the first child in each group where the peanuts are scoops one up in his spoon, runs to the far end, deposits it in the empty bowl and runs back for the second and later the third. Then the first child in each of the other two groups does the same thing, transferring the peanuts back to the first bowl and so on through the team.

Anyone who drops a peanut must pick it up, put it back in the bowl from which he took it and start again. The team which finishes first is the winner.

Pillar Boxes (age ten upwards)

Prepare six shoe boxes by cutting a hole in the lid and writing on each the name of a different county. Station them as widely spread as possible over the house and garden – the more you can spread them out the more strenuous the game. Now cut out about six slips of paper for each guest and write on each the names of fairly well-known towns which lie in the six counties already chosen. You can have the same town on several slips. Fold them over and put into a central box which is the Sorting Office.

At the word 'Go' the children run to the Sorting Office, take out a slip, write their name on it and put it in the correct county box. They then run back to the Sorting Office for another. They must only take one slip at a time.

When all the slips have gone, the pillar boxes are gathered up, the slips checked and the player with the highest number of correctly placed slips receives a prize.

Statues (age four upwards)

Not exactly a new game but one which is still fun to play and can be very pretty to watch.

You need a record player, piano or radio, and can let the children decide whether they want to go solo or do it in pairs.

When the music starts they dance and skip around to their hearts' content, but the moment it stops they must stand stock-still just as they are. Anyone who moves or wobbles is disqualified and can help to referee.

Stepping Stones (age five upwards)

Wrap four blocks of wood or four old books in strong paper and seal them firmly with Sellotape. Thus wrapped they will glide satisfactorily over carpet, wood, tiles or linoleum.

Divide the children into two teams and mark starting and finishing lines, which do not have to be very far apart. The first two children put their feet upon two stepping stones with their *backs* towards the finishing line. When you say 'Go' they must lift a foot from one block and push that forwards a little way towards the finishing line with their foot then step onto it and draw the second block forward. It is difficult enough to make progress, but turning round at the finishing line for the return journey is even worse and very amusing to watch. Every foot on the ground means a penalty point, so the team which finishes first only wins if it has the fewer penalties.

Tag (age four upwards)

The old and well-known game of tag has innumerable variations.

Basically one child starts off as the chaser and has to try and touch another child who then takes his place.

You can play French tag (where the chaser tries to touch

an awkward part of the other child, such as his knee, ankle or foot, and he must keep one hand on this part while he is chasing the next child), or hopping tag (which means that both the chaser and the chased have to hop), or walking tag (useful if space is short), or shadow tag (when you have to step on the other person's shadow), or all fours tag or bent knees tag.

Twist and Run   (ages five to eight)

Divide the children into two teams and stand them facing each other with plenty of space between each child.

The child at the head of each line has a plate with a ping pong ball or an onion on it. He has to weave down the line in and out of the children and back again to his place, saying to each child 'Your lunch, Sir or Madam'. If he drops the ball or the plate, he must start again.

When he has successfully completed the trip he hands the plate to the second child – and so on.

What's the Time, Mr Wolf?   (ages five to nine)

One child is chosen as Mr Wolf. He prowls around followed by the rest of the children in a group.

One after another they call out 'What's the time, Mr Wolf?' So long as he says any time except twelve o'clock they are safe, but if he says 'twelve o'clock. Dinner time!' they must run for their lives to the edge of the lawn or the edge of the carpet or whatever has been decided on as the 'safe' zone.

If Mr Wolf catches anybody, that child takes his turn at being Mr Wolf.

12. MAGIC AND NOVELTIES

A little magic enhances any children's party but don't make the interlude too long. There are also some trick games which are very amusing.

Black Magic (age seven upwards)

For this you need to brief a member of your family to act as spokesman.

Tell the children that you are possessed of strange and magical powers which enable you to guess what they are thinking. Invite them to select anything at all that they can see and you will tell them what it is, then go out of the room while they decide.

When they are ready the spokesman will call you back and fire questions at you: 'Is it the mirror? Is it the cushion? Is it the sofa?' You will have arranged with him beforehand that the object he asks you about immediately *after* a black object will be the one they have chosen. If you want to confound the clever ones even further you can decide on the *second* object after a black one. Always very intriguing.

Clock Magic   (age eight upwards)

A highly effective trick if you ration it strictly to one performance per party. If pressed to repeat it, you will have to claim that it is so exhausting and demanding that it cannot be performed twice in one day – otherwise they will realize how it is done.

Draw the face of a clock on a piece of paper. Hand it together with a pencil to one of the children and tell him or her to put a ring around one number, a line across the middle and a ring around the number opposite – without letting you see. Then ask her to subtract the smaller number from the larger one and to remember what the answer is but not to tell you. Now ask her to fold the paper up very small so that you cannot possibly see it and to pass it to you.

With closed eyes and an aura of fierce concentration press the folded paper against your forehead for a few moments, then open eyes and announce proudly that the answer is six.

Of course it is: any of the small numbers on a clock face subtracted from its opposite larger number leaves six – so pass quickly on to your next item!

Elusive Halfpenny   (age seven upwards)

Now we are getting into the rather more professional sort of magic and you will have to practise this one beforehand. You will appear to transfer magically a halfpenny from your handkerchief to the inside of an orange.

You will need a man's handkerchief with a halfpenny pushed into the hem, a large table knife with a small piece of soft chewing gum stuck on the underside of the blade, about 1″ from the tip, and a bowl of oranges, so that a spectator can select any one at random.

Place a halfpenny on the table and ask for a volunteer from the audience to come out, choose an orange and act as your assistant. Shake open your handkerchief on to the table (but keep hold of the corner with your halfpenny in) and pretend to put the other halfpenny in it and fold the handkerchief around it but, in fact, you keep the halfpenny hidden in your hand. Ask the assistant to feel the folded hankie to confirm that the coin is still there.

Now pick up the knife and make a show of testing the edge of the blade while in fact you are pressing the halfpenny in your hand on to the gum on the back side. Slice the orange in half using the middle (not the tip) of the knife. Open the orange as you drag the knife through. Dragging the knife through will leave the coin in the centre of it. Hand the closed orange to your assistant who will open it and find the halfpenny inside.

Even Blacker Magic (age eight upwards)

Unknown to the others, you must have an accomplice among the children to work this.

Put a glass upside down on a table and invite any of the children to place something inside it while you are out of the room. Say that when you return you will be able to find out who put it there.

When they call you back, lay one finger on the bottom of the upturned glass and ask all the children to do the same one at a time, so that you can 'read their thoughts'.

Your accomplice has to watch carefully and place *his* finger on the glass immediately *after* the person who placed the object inside the glass. Let all the children have a chance to put their fingers on the glass with yours and then announce who the person was.

Famous Names (age nine upwards)

A blatant cheat but effective so long as you remember to destroy the evidence immediately after your performance.

You will need a small jotting pad, a bowl or hat and a slate or large piece of paper.

Invite the children to give you the names of ten famous people. The first child might say 'Winston Churchill' so you write that on a slip of paper, fold it over and drop it in the hat. The second child might say 'Napoleon' but you again write Winston Churchill without, of course, letting them see what you are writing, fold it over and drop it in the hat. Repeat the process for all ten names.

Now you make your prediction by taking the slate or large paper and, without letting the children see what you are putting, write 'Winston Churchill' (how *did* you guess?) upon it and prop it up where the audience can see the paper but not what is written on it.

Shuffle the slips of paper in the hat and invite one of the children to choose one and read it out. After he has done so turn your paper around to show that the name selected was the same.

Magic Box (age nine upwards)

You can perform this simple trick with a packet containing five cigarettes or a box containing five matches, chocolates sweets or nuts. You need a small square or rectangular tray and a member of your family who is 'in the know'.

Hold up the box to the audience and invite any member

to take out as many of its contents as they wish. Without touching the box, you will be able to tell how many have been removed.

Put the box on the tray which your assistant is holding and let her take it to someone in the audience. You must turn away while the chosen member extracts the number he wants. Your assistant retrieves the box and says to you: 'You can turn round now.' He puts the box back on the tray and brings the tray to your table. You look at the box and then pace around in a preoccupied way telling the child who has the things to concentrate hard on the number he has taken so that the answer will be transmitted to you.

In fact you know the answer already because you and your assistant have mentally divided the tray into five sections beforehand. If he has replaced the box in the corner nearest to his right hand, one has been removed; if it is in the corner nearest to his left hand, two have been taken; the front left corner is three, the front right corner four and the centre five.

Magic Dice (age eight upwards)

This is another trick which you can only perform once at any gathering so when it is done pass quickly on to something else. You need three dice, a piece of notepaper and a pencil.

Hand the dice to one of the spectators, ask him to roll them and add together the three topmost numbers without telling you what they are. You turn away to write down your prediction on the piece of paper which you fold and hand to another spectator for safe keeping. When the first child has added up the top numbers tell him to pick up each dice and add to his first total the total of the numbers on the bottom. When he has his final total ask him to announce it and then ask the spectator holding the paper to unfold it and read out what is written. It will be the same number.

The explanation is simple. The opposite faces of any dice add up to seven (one is opposite six, two is opposite five, three is opposite four). Therefore the numbers on the top plus the numbers on the bottom will always add up to twenty-one. The magician thus knows the result in advance and merely writes twenty-one on his piece of paper.

It is important that the spectator counts the three top numbers first and then the three bottom ones. If he picks up each dice in turn he will notice that each adds up to seven.

Match Magic (age eight upwards)

You need two matchboxes, marked 'A' and 'B'. 'A' will contain one more (used) match than 'B'.

Ask a child in the audience to take the same number of matches from each box while you turn away. He can take any number so long as it is not more than half. Then ask him to take eight matches from 'A' and put them in his pocket (which is why you should have used matches). Now ask him to count the number left in 'A' and, without telling you, take that number out of 'B'.

Turn around and, placing a thoughtful finger upon 'B', you announce that in box 'B' he will find exactly seven matches. You will be right because there will *always* be one less than you told him to take away from 'A'. You don't necessarily have to ask him to extract eight but however many you ask him to take will be one more than the final answer.

Nelson's Eye (age nine upwards)

This is not for the squeamish but it always makes a big impression on a fairly robust group. It is probably best to have one of your own children to act as Nelson, for secrecy is the key to success. Nelson is prepared in another room by donning some sort of hard hat and taking one arm out of his jacket so that the sleeve hangs empty. Then you go into the room where the rest of the children are and say:

'Now I have a big surprise for you. Lord Nelson has turned up. Who'd like to be introduced to Lord Nelson?'

You blindfold the first volunteer and lead him out to where Nelson is waiting. Take the volunteer's hand and run it over Nelson's hat saying:

'This is Lord Nelson's hat.'

Then you feel the good arm and say:

'This is Lord Nelson's good arm.'

You feel the empty sleeve and say:

'This is the arm Lord Nelson lost at the Battle of Trafalgar.'

Then run their fingertips over one of Nelson's (closed, for safety) eyes and say:

'This is Lord Nelson's good eye.' Finally take hold of their first finger and, saying, 'This is Lord Nelson's bad eye,' push it into a half tomato or half orange which Nelson is holding up at eye level.

Pretty ghoulish but it always brings the house down, and the first victims take a fiendish delight in watching the remaining volunteers.

Penny Puzzle (age seven upwards)

All you need for this amusing trick is a coin, a tumbler and some volunteers.

Ask the volunteers to leave the room, so that they will not see how the others solve the problem. You can explain the trick to the remaining children and then call in the first volunteer.

Seat him at a table with the tumbler in front of him and explain that you are going to press the coin against his forehead so that it sticks and then, when the child who is appointed time-keeper says 'Now', he is to try and shake the coin off into the tumbler. Tell him that whoever gets the coin into the tumbler in the shortest time will be the winner.

Press the coin firmly against the victim's forehead and, when the time-keeper says 'Now', take your hand away but, unknown to the victim, take the coin with it. He will still 'feel' it sticking to his forehead and will give much amusement to the onlookers with his increasingly frantic attempts to dislodge it.

Rescue him fairly quickly, explain and let him enjoy watching the next victim.

Silly Steeplechases   (age seven upwards)

For this you prepare a short obstacle course with cushions, books, plastic buckets, a length of wool to pass under, etc.

Ask for a few volunteers to study the course carefully as they must negotiate it blindfold. Then all but the first leave the room, and once he is blindfolded the obstacles are very quietly removed. It is extremely funny to watch the victims circumnavigating objects that are no longer there.

METRIC CONVERSION TABLES
Weights and Measures

Liquid Measures

British

1 quart	=	2 pints	=	40 fl oz
1 pint	=	4 gills	=	20 fl oz
½ pint	=	2 gills or 1 cup	=	10 fl oz
¼ pint	=	8 tablespoons	=	5 fl oz
		1 tablespoon	=	just over ½ fl oz
		1 dessertspoon	=	⅓ fl oz
		1 teaspoon	=	⅛ fl oz

Metric

1 litre = 10 decilitres (dl) = 100 centilitres (cl) = 1000 millilitres (ml)

Approximate equivalents:

British	Metric	British	Metric
1 quart	1·1 litre	35 fl oz	1 litre
1 pint	6 dl	18 fl oz	½ litre (5 dl)
½ pint	3 dl	9 fl oz	¼ litre (2·5 dl)
¼ pint (1 gill)	1·5 dl	4 fl oz	1 dl
1 tablespoon	15 ml		
1 dessertspoon	10 ml		
1 teaspoon	5 ml		

American

1 quart	=	2 pints	=	32 fl oz
1 pint	=	2 cups	=	16 fl oz
		1 cup	=	8 fl oz
		1 tablespoon	=	½ fl oz
		1 teaspoon	=	⅙ fl oz

Approximate equivalents:

British	American	British	American
1 quart	2½ pints	1½ pints + 3 tbs	1 quart
1 pint	1¼ pints	(32 fl oz)	
½ pint	10 fl oz (1¼ cups)	¾ pint + 2 tbs	1 pint
¼ pint (1 gill)	5 fl oz	(16 fl oz)	
1 tablespoon	1½ tablespoons	½ pint − 2 tbs	1 cup
1 dessertspoon	1 tablespoon	(8 fl oz)	
1 teaspoon	⅓ fl oz		

Solid Measures

British	Metric
16 oz = 1 lb	1000 grammes (g) = 1 kilogramme (kilo)

Approximate equivalents:

British	Metric	British	Metric
1 lb (16 oz)	450 g	2 lb 3 oz	1 kilo (1000 g)
½ lb (8 oz)	225 g	1 lb 2 oz	½ kilo (500 g)
¼ lb (4 oz)	100 g	9 oz	¼ kilo (250 g)
1 oz	25 g	4 oz	100 g

Temperature Equivalents for Oven Thermostat Markings

Fahrenheit	Gas Mark	Centigrade	Heat of Oven
225°F	¼	110°C	Very cool
250°F	½	130°C	Very cool
275°F	1	140°C	Cool
300°F	2	150°C	Cool
325°F	3	170°C	Moderate
350°F	4	180°C	Moderate
375°F	5	190°C	Fairly hot
400°F	6	200°C	Fairly hot
425°F	7	220°C	Hot
450°F	8	230°C	Very hot
475°F	9	240°C	Very hot

INDEX